What is Grammar?

Here's an old children's rhyme about the eight parts of speech of English grammar. It gives you an idea of what grammar is about. Read and remember it.

Noun

Adjective

Preposition

Conjunction

Pronoun

Verb

Adverb

Interjection

Every name is called a **noun**,
As *field* and *fountain, street* and *town*.
In place of noun the **pronoun** stands,
As *he* and *she* can clap their hands.
The **adjective** describes a thing,
As *magic* wand or *bridal* ring.
Most **verbs** mean action, something done,
To *read* and *write*, to *jump* and *run*.
How things are done the **adverbs** tell,
As *quickly, slowly, badly, well.*
The **preposition** shows relation,
As *in* the street or *at* the station.
Conjunctions join, in many ways,
Sentences, words, *or* phrase *and* phrase.
The **interjection** cries out, "*Heed!*
An exclamation point must
follow me!"

5

2 The Capital Letter

The **capital letter** is also called a **big letter** or **upper-case** letter, or sometimes just a **capital**.

A   B   C   D   E   F   G   H   I   J   K   L   M

N   O   P   Q   R   S   T   U   V   W   X   Y   Z

When do you use a capital letter?

4 Use a capital letter for the first letter in a
   sentence:
       The dog is barking.
       Come here!

4 Always use a capital letter for the word **I**:
       I am eight years old.
       Tom and I are good friends.

4 Use a capital letter for the names of people:
       Alice, Tom, James, Kim, Snow White

4 Use a capital letter for the names of places:
       National Museum, Bronx Zoo, London, Sacramento

4 Use a capital letter for festivals, holidays,
   days of the week, months of the year:
New Year's Day, Christmas, Labor Day, Mother's Day,
Sunday, Monday, Friday, January, May, July, October

Exercise 1

Circle the letters that should be CAPITALS. Then write the correct letter in the space above them.

1 peter and i are good friends.

2 we are going to chicago during our summer vacation.

3 there is an interesting football game on sunday.

4 jason lives on thomson avenue.

   january is the first month of the year.

Exercise 2

Look at the signs on the left. Can you find the mistakes? Write the names correctly.

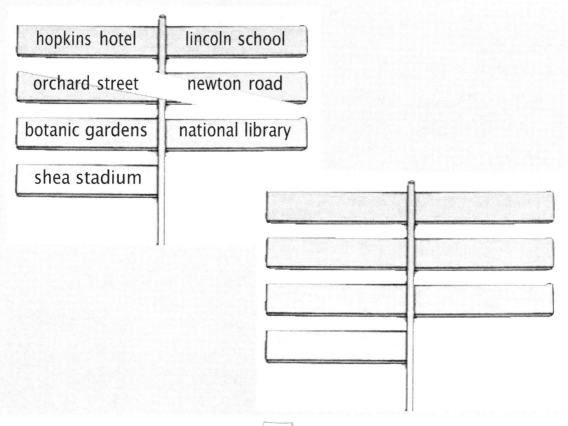

hopkins hotel   lincoln school

orchard street   newton road

botanic gardens   national library

shea stadium

3 Nouns

Common Nouns

> **Nouns** are divided into **common nouns** and **proper nouns**.
> **Common nouns** are words for people, animals, places, or things.
>
> These are words for people. They are common nouns.

artist

clown

acrobat

Word File

Here are more words for people:

actor	lawyer
aunt	judge
baby	man
baker	nurse
cook	police officer
dentist	singer
doctor	soldier
giant	teacher

astronaut

Did you know?

Another word for **astronaut** is **spaceman** or **spacewoman**.

A Book FOR

BASIC ENGLISH GRAMMAR

(ESL)

ENGLISH AS THE SECOND LANGUAGE SPEAKERS

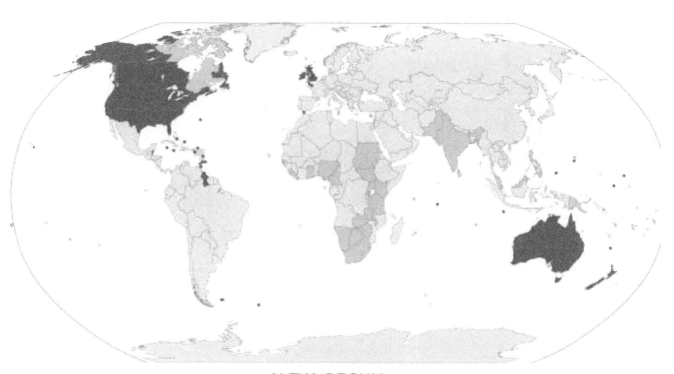

ALEYA BEGUM

BASIC ENGLISH GRAMMAR

(ESL) English as the Second Language

What You'll Find in this Book

This page is internationally blank

These are words for animals. They are common nouns.

eagle

zebra

deer

bird

crocodile

bear

Word File

Here are more words for animals:

cat	goose
cow	hen
dog	horse
dolphin	mouse
duck	parrot
fish	shark
goat	whale

These are words for places. They are common nouns.

beach

park

library

shop

Word File

Here are more words for places:

airport	market
cave	mountain
church	playground
farm	restaurant
hill	school
hospital	seashore
hotel	stadium
house	supermarket
island	temple
mall	zoo

These are words for things. They are common nouns.

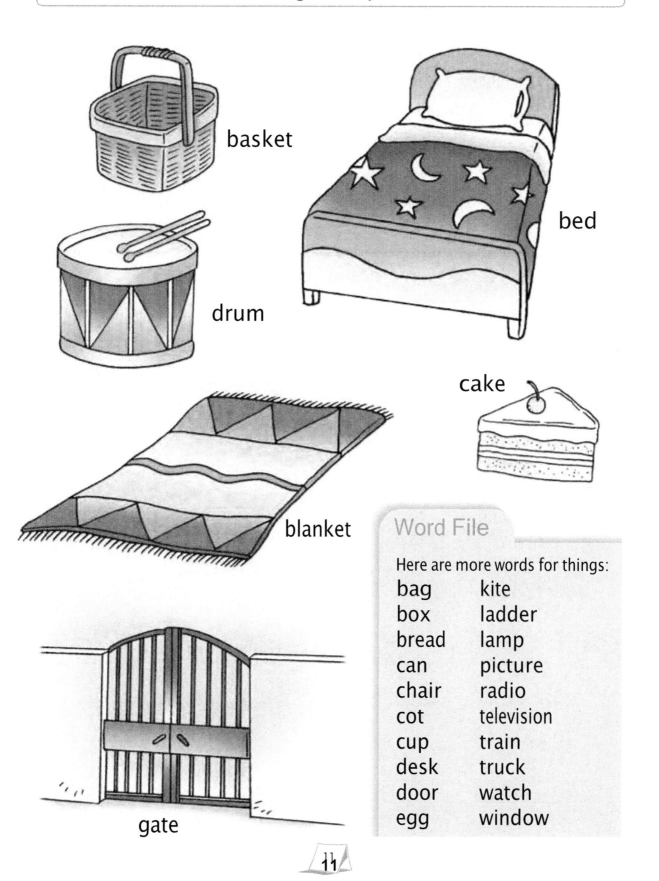

basket

bed

drum

cake

blanket

gate

Word File

Here are more words for things:

bag	kite
box	ladder
bread	lamp
can	picture
chair	radio
cot	television
cup	train
desk	truck
door	watch
egg	window

Exercise 1

Underline the common nouns in these sentences.

1. There's a little bird in the garden.
2. Who is your teacher?
3. Don't eat that rotten apple.
4. Kate has a lovely doll.
5. I like reading stories.
6. My father is a doctor.
7. Every child has a dictionary.
8. Rudy hates bananas.
9. The phone is ringing.
10. Here's a book for you.

Exercise 2

Here's a mixed bag of words. Put each word under its correct heading.

swimmer	snail	fire engine	clown
letters	flag	river	barber
mountain	fox	hotel	parrot
granny	taxi	gardener	camel

People	Animals	Places	Things
_____	_____	_____	_____
_____	_____	_____	_____
_____	_____	_____	_____
_____	_____	_____	_____
_____	_____	_____	_____

Proper Nouns

Proper nouns are names for particular people, places or things. They always begin with a capital letter.

Omar

Beethoven

Santa Claus

Lisa

Word File

Here are some more names of people:

Ali Baba
Florence Nightingale
Derek Jeter
Pauline
Johnny Depp
Patrick
Harry Potter
Pinocchio
Robin Hood

Your own name and the names of your friends are proper nouns too.

Kim Lee

The names of countries and their people are also proper nouns.

| American | Egyptian | Indian | Italian | Thai |

| Japanese | Korean | Malay | Filipino | Pakistani |

Country	People	Country	People
America	Americans	Korea	Koreans
Egypt	Egyptians	Malaysia	Malaysians
India	Indians	Pakistan	Pakistanis
Italy	Italians	France	the French
Japan	the Japanese	Thailand	Thais

The names of towns, cities, buildings and landmarks are proper nouns.

Hong Kong

Egypt

the Great Wall of China

the Statue of Liberty

Tokyo

Sydney

Bangkok	New Delhi	
London	Denver	the Grand Canyon
New York	Central Park	the Leaning Tower of Pisa
Paris	the Eiffel Tower	Brooklyn Bridge
Beijing	Big Ben	Pike's Peak

The days of the week and months of the year are proper nouns.

Days
Sunday
Monday
Tuesday
Wednesday
Thursday
Friday
Saturday

Months
January
February
March
April
May
June
July
August
September
October
November
December

January is the first month of the year.

Sunday is the first day of the week.

A table that shows the months, weeks days

The names of mountains, seas, rivers and lakes are proper nouns.

Mount Everest

the Thames

Lake Michigan
the Alps   the Himalayas
the Dead Sea   the Pacific Ocean   Niagara Falls
Mount Fuji   the Yellow River

Did you know?

You often use **the** before names of oceans, rivers, seas and ranges of mountains.

Mount means **mountain**.
It is often used in the names of mountains.

For example: Mount Everest
                Mount St. Helens

The written short form for **Mount** is **Mt.**
For example: Mt. Everest, Mt. Fuji

The names of festivals, some special events and holidays are proper nouns, too.

Valentine's Day

Father's Day

Halloween

New Year's Day

Word File

Here are more names of festivals and holidays:

Christmas	Mother's Day
Memorial Day	April Fool's Day
Labor Day	Thanksgiving Day
Independence Day	St. Patrick's Day

Exercise 1

Underline the *proper nouns* in the following sentences.

1 July is often the hottest month in summer.

2 One day Ali Baba saw the forty thieves hiding in a cave.

3 Shawn and Ashley are going to the beach for a swim.

4 Mr. Lee is reading a book.

"I am your fairy godmother," said the old woman to Cinderella.

Uncle Mike is a lawyer.

Next Tuesday is a public holiday.

Many children enjoyed the movie Lion King.

Exercise 2

Look at the words in the box. Which ones are *common nouns* and which ones are *proper nouns*? Put each word under its correct heading.

Lisa	bank	President Hotel	United Bank
January	beach	White Sand Beach	hotel
doctor	month	Dr. Wang	girl

Common Nouns	Proper Nouns
_____	_____
_____	_____
_____	_____
_____	_____
_____	_____

Exercise 3

Write **C** for *common* or **P** for *proper* on the blank before each noun.

1. _____ the White House
2. _____ the green dress
3. _____ the tall building
4. _____ the Empire State Building
   _____ the Yellow River
   _____ the muddy river
   _____ the governor
   _____ Governor Parker
   _____ the oregon Trail
10. _____ the winding trail

Exercise 4

Underline the nouns that should be capitalized. Circle the nouns that should *not* be capitalized.

1. Robert louis Stevenson wrote treasure island.
2. The Capital of illinois is Springfield.
3. My Friends and I prefer Glittergums toothpaste.
4. Their Family visited Yellowstone national Park.
   Juan and maria attend kennedy Middle school.
   We had a Surprise Party for aunt Helen.
   Spring and Fall are my favorite Seasons.
   The Manager scolded his lazy Employees.

Singular Nouns

Nouns can be **singular** or **plural**. When you are talking about one person, animal, place, or thing, use a singular noun.

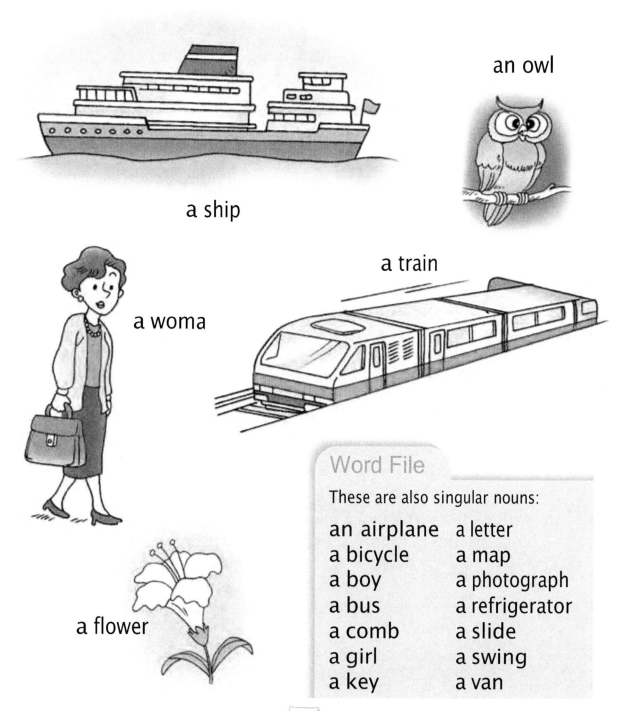

a ship

an owl

a woma

a train

a flower

Word File

These are also singular nouns:

an airplane	a letter
a bicycle	a map
a boy	a photograph
a bus	a refrigerator
a comb	a slide
a girl	a swing
a key	a van

4 Use **a** or **an** before singular nouns.
Use **an** before words beginning with **vowels**
(a, e, i, o, u). For example, say:

an axe	**an** igloo
an egg	**an** orange
an envelope	**an** umbrella
an ice cream	**an** uncle

4 But some words don't follow this rule. For example,
use **a** (not **an**) before these words that begin with **u**:

    a uniform   **a** university

4 Use **a** before words beginning with the other
letters of the alphabet, called **consonants**.
For example, say:

a basket	**a** rainbow
a bowl	**a** monster
a car	**a** pillow
a hill	**a** watch
a house	**a** zoo

4 But some words don't follow this rule. For example,
use **an** (not **a**) before these words that begin with **h**:

    an heir
    an honor
    an hour

Plural Nouns

When you are talking about two or more people, animals, places, or things, use plural nouns.
Most nouns are made plural by adding **-s** at the end.

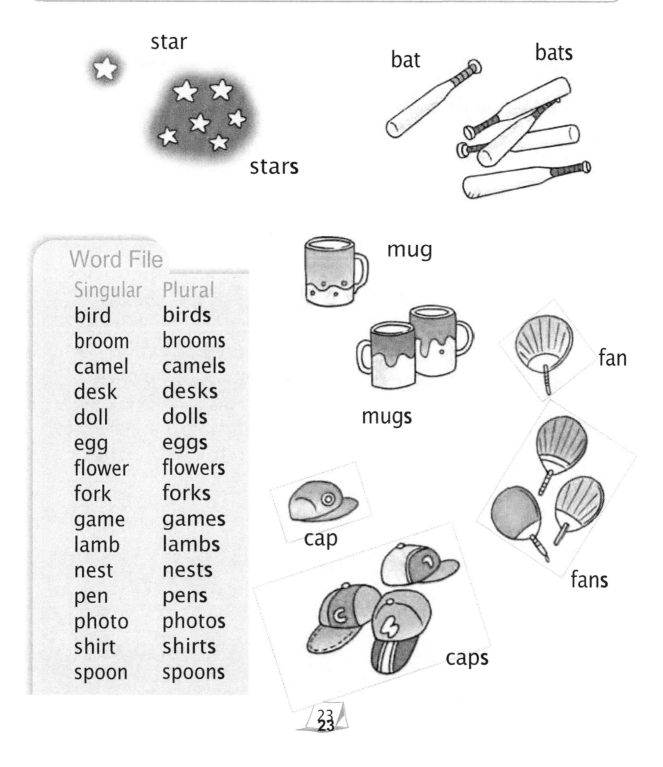

star

stars

bat

bats

mug

mugs

fan

fans

cap

caps

Word File

Singular	Plural
bird	birds
broom	brooms
camel	camels
desk	desks
doll	dolls
egg	eggs
flower	flowers
fork	forks
game	games
lamb	lambs
nest	nests
pen	pens
photo	photos
shirt	shirts
spoon	spoons

Some plural nouns end in -**es**.

bus

buses

glass

glasses

brush

brushes

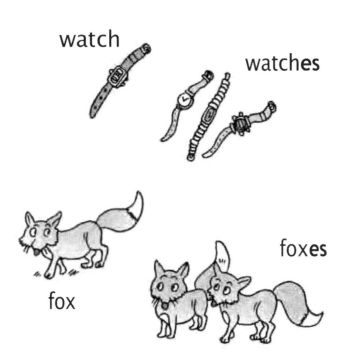

watch

watches

fox

foxes

Word File

Singular	Plural
beach	beaches
branch	branches
box	boxes
bush	bushes
church	churches
dish	dishes
dress	dresses
sandwich	sandwiches
witch	witches

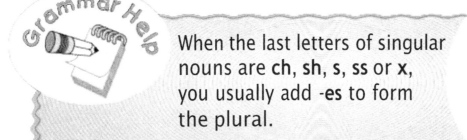

Grammar Help

When the last letters of singular nouns are **ch**, **sh**, **s**, **ss** or **x**, you usually add -**es** to form the plural.

ch
sh
s
ss
x
+ es

Some plural nouns end in **-ies**.

butterfl**ies**

butterfly

canar**ies**

canary

Word File	
Singular	Plural
baby	bab**ies**
cherry	cherr**ies**
diary	diar**ies**
dictionary	dictionar**ies**
fairy	fair**ies**
family	famil**ies**
fly	fl**ies**
lady	lad**ies**
library	librar**ies**
puppy	pupp**ies**
story	stor**ies**
strawberry	strawberr**ies**

lil**ies**

lily

cand**ies**

candy

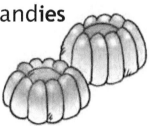

Grammar Help

Nouns like these are made plural by changing **y** to **i**, and adding **-es**.

What if there is a vowel before the **y**?
In that case, add **-s** to form the plural.

key

turkey

keys

turkeys

tray

trays

Word File

Singular	Plural
chimney	chimneys
cowboy	cowboys
day	days
donkey	donkeys
jersey	jerseys
kidney	kidneys
monkey	monkeys
toy	toys
trolley	trolleys
valley	valleys

If a noun ends in **-f**, you often change **f** to **v**, and add **-es**.

Singular	Plural	Singular	Plural
calf	cal**ves**	loaf	loa**ves**
elf	el**ves**	shelf	shel**ves**
half	hal**ves**	thief	thie**ves**
leaf	lea**ves**	wolf	wo**lves**

Grammar Help

often nouns that end in **-f**, just need **-s** to form the plural.

Singular	Plural	Singular	Plural
chef	chef**s**	handkerchief	handkerchief**s**
chief	chief**s**	roof	roof**s**
cliff	cliff**s**	sheriff	sheriff**s**

For some words that end in **-f**, the plural can be spelled in two different ways.

Singular	Plural
dwarf	dwarf**s** or dwar**ves**
hoof	hoof**s** or hoo**ves**
scarf	scarf**s** or scar**ves**

With some words that end in **-fe**, you change **f** to **v**, and add **-s**.

Singular	Plural
knife	kni**ves**
life	li**ves**
wife	wi**ves**

Did you know?

But you only add **-s** to **giraffe** to form the plural.

27

If a noun ends in -**o**, you just add -**s** to form the plural.

 a rhino  rhino**s**

a kangaroo   kangaroo**s**

Word File

Singular	Plural
a hippo	hippo**s**
a video	video**s**
a zoo	zoo**s**

But with some nouns that end in -**o**, you add -**es** to form the plural.

 a flamingo

flamingo**es**

Word File

Singular	Plural
a tomato	tomato**es**
a potato	potato**es**
a hero	hero**es**

 *Grammar Help*

With some nouns that end in -**o**, you can add either -**s** or -**es** to form the plural.

Singular	Plural	Plural
a mango	mango**es**	mango**s**
a mosquito	mosquito**es**	mosquito**s**
a zero	zero**es**	zero**s**
a buffalo	buffalo**es**	buffalo**s**

Some plural nouns don't follow the **-s** rule. They don't end in **-s**, **-es**, **-ies** or **-ves**. Instead, the word changes form.

mouse

mice

goose

geese

Word File

Singular	Plural
child	children
man	men
ox	oxen
tooth	teeth
woman	women

foot

feet

Did you know?

The plural of the **mouse** that you use with your computer is either **mice** or **mouses**.

29

Some plural nouns are the same as the singular noun.

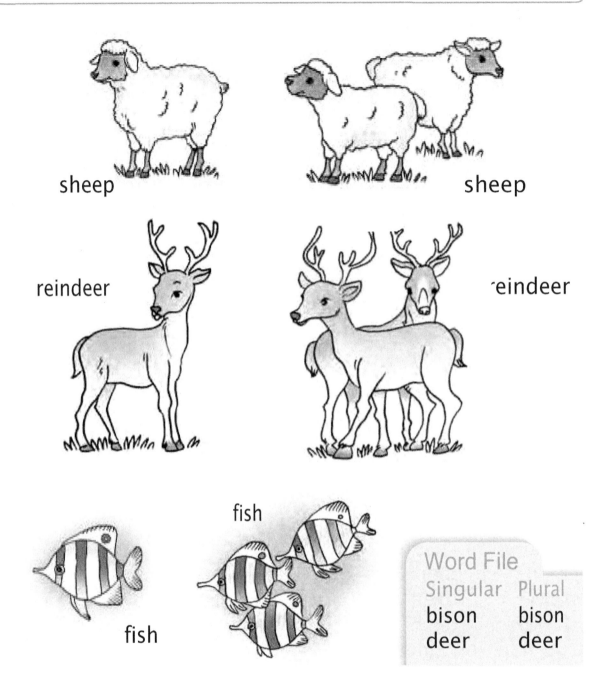

sheep

sheep

reindeer

reindeer

fish

fish

fish

Word File	
Singular	Plural
bison	bison
deer	deer

Did you know?

You can use **fishes** as the plural of **fish** when you are talking about different kinds of fish: all the **fishes** of the Pacific Ocean.

Some nouns are always plural.

binoculars

goggles

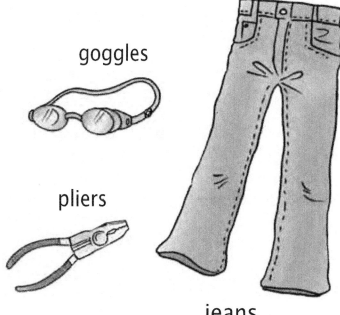

pliers

jeans

Did you know?

Another word for **spectacles** is **glasses**.

spectacles

Grammar Help

You can make these plural nouns singular by using **a pair of**:

a pair of binoculars
a pair of spectacles
a pair of goggles
a pair of jeans
a pair of shorts
a pair of pliers

a pair of shoes

Exercise 1

Look at the words below. Do you know which ones are *singular* and which are *plural*? Put a checkmark (✓) in the correct box.

	Singular	Plural
word		
pencils		
books		
fan		
hat		
children		
kites		
people		
crab		
foxes		

Exercise 2

Do you add *-s* or *-es* to these singular nouns to make them plural? Write your answers on the lines.

Singular	Plural		Singular	Plural
1 desk	_____	6 basket	_____
2 class	_____	7 peach	_____
3 comb	_____	8 belt	_____
4 mug	_____	9 taxi	_____
5 bus	_____	10 box	_____

Exercise 3

Do you change -y to -ies, or just add -s to make these singular nouns plural? Write your anwers.

Singular	Plural	Singular	Plural
1 key	_____	6 toy	_____
2 city	_____	7 baby	_____
3 butterfly	_____	8 party	_____
4 monkey	_____	9 chimney	_____
5 fly	_____	10 lady	_____

Exercise 4

All these singular nouns end with -o. Add either -s or -es as you write the plurals on the line.

Singular	Plural	Singular	Plural
1 video	_____	6 radio	_____
2 piano	_____	7 hippo	_____
3 mango	_____	8 zoo	_____
4 kangaroo	_____	9 zero	_____
5 rhino	_____	10 photo	_____

Collective Nouns

Collective **nouns** are words for groups of people, animals or things.

These are nouns for groups of people.

a family

a crew

an orchestra

Word File
Here are some more groups of people:

an audience	a gang
a band	a group
a choir	a team
a class	

Grammar Help

Many **collective nouns** can be used with a singular or plural verb.
For example:

My family **was** happy to see me.
or
My family **were** happy to see me.

But the following collective nouns always take a plural verb:

cattle   people   the police

Here are more collective nouns that are used for groups of people, animals or things.

a **band** of musicians

a **brood** of chickens

a **school** of fish

Word File

Here are some more collective nouns:

a **bunch** of keys
a **class** of pupils
a **collection** of books
a **deck** of cards
a **fleet** of ships
a **flock** of sheep
a **gaggle** of geese
a **gang** of robbers
a **herd** of cattle
a **litter** of cubs
a **pod** of whales
a **pack** of wolves
a **pride** of lions
a **set** of stamps
a **swarm** of bees
a **troupe** of actors

a **team** of players

a **flight** of steps

Exercise

Farmer John had *several different* kinds of animals on his farm. Write the correct *collective* noun for each group of his animals.

Farmer John had:

a _____ of geese

a _____ of sheep

a _____ of cattle

a _____ of horses

one day a _____ of coyotes tried to attack his animals. Farmer John yelled and waved a pitchfork to frighten them away.

Masculine and Feminine Nouns

Masculine nouns are words for men and boys, and male animals.

Feminine nouns are words for women and girls, and female animals.

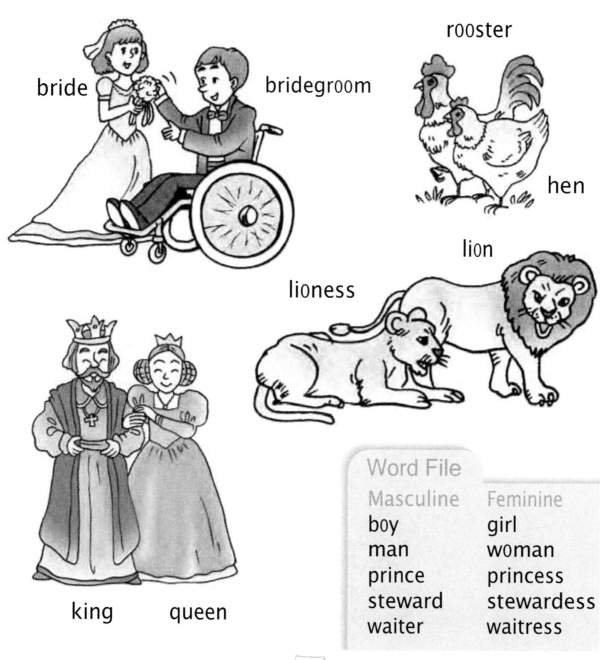

bride

bridegroom

rooster

hen

lion

lioness

king   queen

Word File

Masculine	Feminine
boy	girl
man	woman
prince	princess
steward	stewardess
waiter	waitress

Here are some more masculine and feminine nouns for people.

Masculine

Feminine

Masculine	Feminine
actor	actress
brother	sister
emperor	empress
father	mother
gentleman	lady
grandfather	grandmother
grandson	granddaughter
headmaster	headmistress
man	woman
master	mistress
nephew	niece
prince	princess
son	daughter
steward	stewardess
uncle	aunt
wizard	witch

Did you know?

Masculine nouns belong to the **masculine gender.**
Feminine nouns belong to the **feminine gender.**

Here are some masculine and feminine nouns for male and female animals.

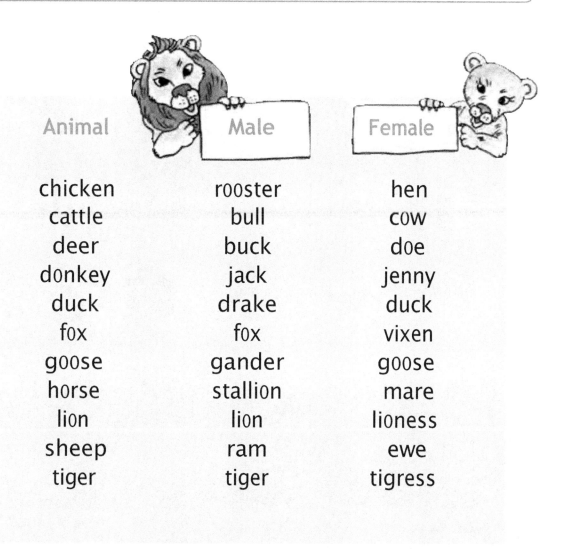

Animal	Male	Female
chicken	rooster	hen
cattle	bull	cow
deer	buck	doe
donkey	jack	jenny
duck	drake	duck
fox	fox	vixen
goose	gander	goose
horse	stallion	mare
lion	lion	lioness
sheep	ram	ewe
tiger	tiger	tigress

Nouns that end in **-ess** and **-ress** often belong to the feminine gender. For example:

act**ress**	steward**ess**
lion**ess**	tig**ress**
prince**ss**	wait**ress**

Many nouns are used for both males and females.

doctors

dancers

scientists

hairdressers

Grammar Help

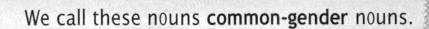

We call these nouns **common-gender** nouns.

Words for things that are neither male nor female are called **neuter nouns**.

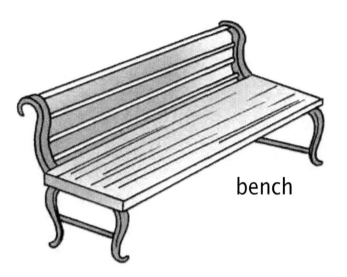
bench

leaves

mirror

fire

waterfall

Word File

Here are some neuter nouns:

ball	forest
building	gymnasium
broom	playground
cake	rock
computer	sky
card	socks
floor	wind

Exercise 1

Fill in the blanks with the correct *masculine* or *feminine* nouns.

Masculine	Feminine
1 master	_____
2 uncle	_____
3 _____	niece
4 _____	lioness
5 tiger	_____
6 _____	empress
7 husband	_____
8 son	_____
9 _____	mother
10 _____	madam

Exercise 2

Fill in each blank with a suitable *masculine* or *feminine* noun.

1 The host and the _____ welcomed their guests.

2 The steward and the _____ look after the passengers on the plane.

3 My uncle and _____ lived in Nebraska.

4 The king and the _____ had two children, a boy and a _____. The prince was eight and the _____ was five.

5 Ladies and _____ , welcome to our party this evening.

Exercise 3

Look at the words in the box. Write each word under its correct heading.

children	sun	witch	king
boy	son	father	girl
mother	queen	file	teacher
lamp	doctor	dancer	wizard
ram	rooster	elf	fish

Masculine	Feminine	Common Gender	Neuter

4 Pronouns

A **pronoun** is a word that takes the place of a common noun or a proper noun. There are different kinds of pronouns.

Personal Pronouns

The words **I**, **you**, **he**, **she**, **it**, **we** and **they** are called **personal pronouns**. They take the place of nouns and are used as the **subject** of the verb in a sentence.

My name is **David**. I am the youngest in the family.

This is **my father**. He is a teacher.

This is **my mother**. She is a lawyer.

I have **a brother** and **two sisters**.

They are Peter, Sharon and Jenny.

I have **a dog**. It is called Lucky.

Lucky, you are a good dog.

Good morning, **children**! You may sit down now.

My family and I live in a big city. We have an apartment.

The **subject** of a sentence is the person, animal, place or thing that does the action shown by the verb.

The words **me**, **you**, **him**, **her**, **it**, **us** and **them** are also personal pronouns. They also take the place of nouns.

These pronouns are used as the **object** of the verb in a sentence.

I am standing on my head. Look at me.

My mother is kind. Everybody likes her.

Lisa, I told you to tidy your bed!

Sharon and Jenny! Dad is waiting for you!

Lucky and I are playing in the park. Dad is watching us.

You must not play with **the knife**. Give it to me.

Pick up **your toys** and put them away.

Baby birds cannot fly.
Mother bird has to feed them.

Tom likes riding **my bicycle**.
I sometimes lend it to him.

Grammar Help

The **object** of a sentence is the person, animal, place or thing that receives the action shown by the verb.

There are three groups of pronouns: **first person**, **second person** and **third person**.

The **person speaking** is called the **first person**. The first-person pronouns are **I** or **me** (in the singular) and **we** or **us** (in the plural).

The **person spoken to** is called the **second person**. The second-person pronoun is **you** (in both singular and plural).

The **person** (or **animal**, or **thing**) **spoken about** is called the **third person**. The third-person pronouns are **he** or **him**, **she** or **her**, and **it** (in the singular), and **they** or **them** (in the plural).

The word **I** is always spelled with a capital letter. The pronoun **he** is used for men and boys, **she** for women and girls, and **it** for things and animals.

Here is a table to help you.

	Subject	Object
First person singular	I	me
Second person singular	you	you
Third person singular	he	him
	she	her
	it	it
First person plural	we	us
Second person plural	you	you
Third person plural	they	them

Reflexive Pronouns

The words **myself**, **yourself**, **himself**, **herself**, **itself**, **ourselves**, **yourselves** and **themselves** are called **reflexive pronouns**.

They refer to the person or animal that is the subject of the verb.

I made this cake myself.

Be careful with the knife. **You**'ll cut yourself.

Michael is looking at himself in the mirror.

Susan has hurt herself.

Our **cat** washes itself after each meal.

We organized the party all by ourselves.

Come in, **children**, and find yourselves a seat.

Baby birds are too young to look after themselves.

Grammar Help

Here is a table to remind you about reflexive pronouns.

	Singular	Plural
First person	(I, me) myself	(we, us) ourselves
Second person	(you) yourself	(you) yourselves
Third person	(he, him) himself	(they, them) themselves
	(she, her) herself	(they, them) themselves
	(it) itself	(they, them) themselves

Interrogative Pronouns

The words **who**, **whom**, **whose**, **what** and **which** are called interrogative pronouns.

These pronouns are used to ask questions.

Who

Who is he talking to?
Who are those people?

Whom

Whom are you playing with?
Whom is he talking to?

Which

Which of these bags is yours?
Which do you prefer?

Whose

Whose is this umbrella?
Whose are these gloves?

What

What is your dog's name?
What are you talking about?
What is the time?

Grammar Help

Who can be used as the **object** of a verb as well as the **subject**.

Whom is used only as the **object**. For example, you can say:

Who are you playing with?
or
Whom are you playing with?

Demonstrative Pronouns

The words **this**, **these**, **that** and **those** are called **demonstrative pronouns**. They are showing words.

Those are goats.

These are sheep.

This is my house.
This is a hill.
These are donkeys.
What is **this**?
Did you drop **this**?
Hi, Jane! **This** is Michael!

That is John's house.
That is a mountain.
Those are horses.
What are **those**?
We can do better than **that**.
No, **that**'s not mine.
You mean you won?
That's amazing!
Hello, who is **that** speaking, please?
Hello, is **that** you, George?

Grammar Help

You use **this** and **these** when you point to things **near** you.
You use **that** and **those** when you point to things **farther away**.

Demonstrative pronouns can be singular or plural:

Singular	Plural
this	these
that	those

Exercise 1

Draw a line to join each of the *subject pronouns*
to the *object pronoun* that matches.

I   he   it   she   they   you   we

us   her   you   them   me   him   it

Exercise 2

Fill in the blanks with the correct pronouns.

1 Peter and I are brothers. _____ share a bedroom together.

2 Sue isn't well. Dad is taking _____ to see a doctor.

3 My brother is a teacher. _____ teaches English.

4 All his students like _____ very much.

5 Children, _____ are making too much noise!

6 Who are those people? Where are _____ from?

7 Mom is a doctor. _____ works in a hospital.

8 The sky is getting dark. _____ is going to rain.

9 John, we are all waiting for _____. Are you coming with _____?

10 May _____ borrow your pen?

11 Yes, of course. When can you return _____ to _____?

12 What are _____ reading, Jenny?

Exercise 3

Fill in the blanks with the correct *reflexive pronouns* from the box.

yourselves	themselves	itself	myself
himself	yourself	ourselves	herself

1 No one can help us. We have to help _____.

2 Jane always makes the bed by _____.

3 They painted the wall all by _____.

4 I hurt _____ in the playground yesterday.

5 John, you must behave _____ before your friends.

6 Children, you must do the homework _____.

7 Tom defended _____ against the bullies.

8 The dog is scratching _____.

Exercise 4

Write the correct *interrogative pronouns* in the blanks to complete the sentences:

1 _____ is the matter with you?

2 _____ invented the computer?

3 _____ of the twins is older?

4 _____ do you wish to speak to?

5 _____ is this car in front of our house?

6 _____ knows the answer?

7 _____ came first, the chicken or the egg?

8 _____ would you like to drink?

9 _____ of them do you think will win the race?

10 _____ is the word for a stamp collector?

5 Adjectives

An **adjective** is a describing word. It tells you more about a noun. An adjective usually appears before the noun it describes. Sometimes, though, the adjective appears after the noun, later in the sentence.

a **smart** dog

an **old** building

a **tall** basketball player

a **busy** street
a **dark** corner
a **deep** sea
a **large** bed
It is **windy**.
John's handwriting is very **neat**.
The sea is **rough**.
All the players are very **tall**.
The baby's hands are very **small**.
Sue's drawing is **beautiful**.
That problem is too **difficult**.
Peter is very **quiet** today.

a **low** fence

Exercise 1

Underline the *adjectives* in the following sentences.

1 There is an empty room upstairs.

2 It's a hot summer.

3 You are so kind.

4 Don't be crazy.

5 This park is clean and green.

6 Many people exercise to keep healthy.

7 I think these eggs are rotten.

8 We are all bored. There isn't anything to do.

9 The pupils don't find the joke amusing.

10 James was absent because he was ill.

Exercise 2

Fill in the blanks with suitable *adjectives* from the box.

hot	large	short	free
high	sweet	poor	playful

1 The ice cream is very _____.

2 It's very _____ in summer.

3 The company is giving away _____ gifts to its customers.

4 They live in a _____ house.

5 Jean is wearing a _____ skirt.

6 The climbers are climbing up a _____ mountain.

7 These puppies are very _____.

8 Many _____ people have no home.

Adjective Endings

Adjectives have different **endings**.
Some adjectives end in -**ful** or -**less**.

homeless people

playful puppies

a **beautiful** dress
a **careless** driver
a **faithful** dog
a **harmless** insect
a **useful** tool

Grammar Help

An adjective that ends in -**less** is the opposite of the same adjective that ends in -**ful**.
For example:

careful – careless   useful – useless
colorful – colorless   harmful – harmless

The -**ful** ending means **having a lot of something**.
For example:

painful   =   having a lot of pain
hopeful   =   having a lot of hope

The -**less** ending means **without**.
For example:

leafless   =   without leaves
sleeveless =   without sleeves

Some adjectives end in **-y**.

a **dirty** street
a **noisy** room
an **oily** pot
a **sleepy** passenger
a **sunny** day

a **stormy** sea

a **muddy** path

Some adjectives end in **-ive**.

an **expensive** necklace

an **active** child
an **attractive** hat
a **creative** toy

talkative pupils

Some adjectives end in **-ing**.

a **cunning** fox

a **caring** nurse
an **interesting** book
loving parents
matching clothes
a **smiling** face

dazzling sunshine

Some adjectives end in **-ly**.

a **costly** diamond ring
an **elderly** woman
lively kittens
a **lonely** boy
a **lovely** girl
a **weekly** magazine

a **daily** newspaper

a **friendly** police officer

Many **adverbs** also end in **-ly**.

Here are some adjectives with the endings **-able**, **-al**, **-en**, **-ible**, **-ish** and **-ous**.

a **broken** chair

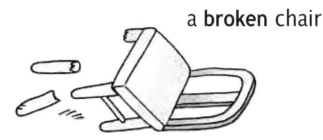

a **famous** pop singer

childish behavior
a **comfortable** chair
a **dangerous** place
a **foolish** act
a **horrible** smell
a **loveable** koala

a **national** costume
a **musical** instrument
a **terrible** mess
a **woolen** sweater
a **wooden** table

a **poisonous** snake

Exercise 1

Add the correct endings to turn these words into *adjectives*.

-y	-ful	-less	-al

1 peace _____

2 storm _____

3 mud _____

4 forget _____

5 spot _____

6 dirt _____

7 music _____

8 nation _____

9 dust _____

10 play _____

Exercise 2

Add the correct endings to turn these words into *adjectives*.

-en	-y	-ing
-ish	-ous	-ly

1 wind _____

2 gold _____

3 friend _____

4 rot _____

5 danger _____

6 fool _____

7 charm _____

8 child _____

9 love _____

10 interest _____

Kinds of Adjectives

There are different kinds of adjectives.
Some adjectives describe the **qualities** of nouns.

a **cold** drink

a **hot** bun

an **ugly** monster

a **fierce** dog

a **beautiful** rainbow
a **clever** monkey
a **difficult** question
happy children
a **kind** lady
a **new** car
an **old** house
a **pretty** girl
a **rich** family
a **sad** story
a **strong** man
a **wicked** queen

a **loud** crash

Some adjectives tell you which place or country a person or thing comes from, or belongs to. They are called **adjectives of origin**.

Chinese kungfu

an **Indian** temple

A **Filipino** shirt

a **Mexican** hat

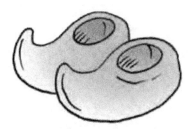

Dutch clogs

Australian apples
a **Balinese** dancer
the **English** language
the **French** flag
an **Italian** car
a **Japanese** garden
a **Scottish** kilt
Thai boxing

Some adjectives tell you the **color** of things.

Please get me some **white** paint.

The sky is **gray**.

The sea is **blue**.
George is wearing **brown** shoes.
I don't like **green** apples.
Carrots are **orange**.
Flamingos are **pink**.
Eggplants are **purple**.
Roses are **red**.

Your hands are **black**!

Some adjectives tell you the **size** of the nouns they describe.

a **huge** balloon

a **big** hat
broad shoulders
a **high** mountain
a **large** ship
a **long** bridge
a **low** ceiling
a **narrow** path
small animals
tiny insects
a **wide** street

a **fat** sumo wrestler

a **thin** boy

a **short** man

Did you know?

The word **tall** describes people and narrow, upright objects. For example, you can say:

a **tall** girl   a **tall** bookcase

The word **high** describes bigger or wider objects that reach a great height. For example, you can say:

a **high** mountain   a **high** wall

Numbers are adjectives, too. They tell you how many people, animals, or things there are. Sometimes they are called **adjectives of quantity**.

one giant

two princes

three princesses

four mermaids

five witches

six fairies

seven elves

nine dwarfs

eight puppets

ten angels

eleven hens
twelve geese
thirteen birds
fourteen mice

fifteen frogs
sixteen snails
seventeen kittens
eighteen ants

nineteen lizards
twenty butterflies

Other adjectives tell you something about quantity without giving you the exact number.

some soldiers

a lot of books

a little ice cream
a little rice
not **many** people
too **much** salt
lots of insects
plenty of money
some food
Is there **any** milk?

a few cups

a few puppies

Did you know?

Adjectives that tell you about **quantity** are also called **quantifying determiners**.

Exercise

Look at the underlined words in the following sentences. Do you know what kinds of adjectives they are?

In the blanks write *C* if the underlined words tell you about *color*, *S* if they tell you about *size*, *Ql* if they tell you about *quality*, *O* if they tell you about *origin*, or *Qn* if they tell you about the *number* or *quantity* of things.

1 Dad has <u>two</u> pairs of shoes. ___

2 one pair is <u>brown</u> and the other pair is <u>black</u>. ___
  ___

3 This is a very <u>simple</u> puzzle. ___

4 What color is the <u>American</u> flag? ___

5 A <u>kind</u> fairy appeared before Cinderella. ___

6 He is a <u>proud</u> man. ___

7 There is <u>some</u> food left. ___

8 Tom is wearing a <u>blue</u> T-shirt. ___

9 Jack has <u>ten</u> marbles; Peter has <u>twenty</u>. ___ ___

10 How <u>many</u> marbles have Jack and Peter altogether? ___

11 There is an <u>Indian</u> temple in the city. ___

12 There is a <u>large</u> crowd outside the temple. ___

13 My house is just <u>a few</u> miles from the school. ___

14 They are driving a <u>small</u> car. ___

15 Sue likes those <u>yellow</u> and <u>red</u> balloons. ___ ___

Comparison of Adjectives

When you compare two people or things, use the **comparative** form of the adjective.

Lots of comparative adjectives end in **-er**.

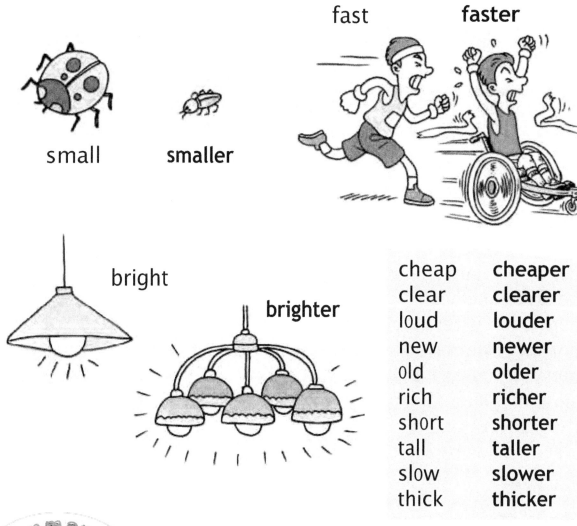

fast   **faster**

small   **smaller**

bright

brighter

cheap	**cheaper**
clear	**clearer**
loud	**louder**
new	**newer**
old	**older**
rich	**richer**
short	**shorter**
tall	**taller**
slow	**slower**
thick	**thicker**

Grammar Help

The word **than** is often used with comparative adjectives. For example, you might say:

Jack is taller **than** John.

A sports car is faster **than** a motorbike.

Use the **superlative** form of an adjective to compare three or more nouns. Lots of superlatives end in -**est**.

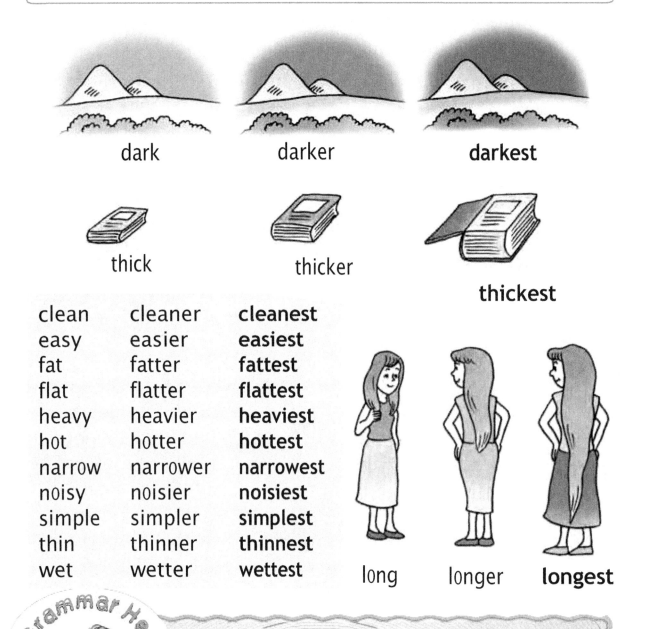

dark   darker   **darkest**

thick   thicker

thickest

clean	cleaner	**cleanest**
easy	easier	**easiest**
fat	fatter	**fattest**
flat	flatter	**flattest**
heavy	heavier	**heaviest**
hot	hotter	**hottest**
narrow	narrower	narrowest
noisy	noisier	**noisiest**
simple	simpler	**simplest**
thin	thinner	**thinnest**
wet	wetter	**wettest**

long   longer   **longest**

Grammar Help

You often add **the** before the superlative form. For example, you say:

Mount Everest is **the** highest mountain in the world.

Peter is **the** tallest boy in his class.

4 With adjectives that end in -**e**, add -**r** to form
the **comparative**, and -**st** to form the **superlative**.
For example:

	Comparative	Superlative
close	clos**er**	clos**est**
large	larg**er**	larg**est**
safe	saf**er**	saf**est**
wide	wid**er**	wid**est**

4 Some adjectives have only one syllable, end with a
consonant, and have a single vowel before the
consonant. With these adjectives, double the last letter
before adding –**er** to form the **comparative**, and -**est** to
form the **superlative**. For example:

	Comparative	Superlative
big	bi**gger**	bi**ggest**
dim	di**mmer**	di**mmest**
mad	ma**dder**	ma**ddest**
sad	sa**dder**	sa**ddest**

4 Some adjectives have two syllables and end in -**y**. With
these adjectives change the **y** to **i**. Then add -**er** to form
the **comparative**, and -**est** to form the **superlative**.
For example:

	Comparative	Superlative
busy	bus**ier**	bus**iest**
dirty	dirt**ier**	dirt**iest**
happy	happ**ier**	happ**iest**
pretty	prett**ier**	prett**iest**

With some adjectives, you use **more** to make the comparative form, and **most** to make the superlative form.

beautiful   **more** beautiful   **most** beautiful

active   **more** active   **most** active
charming   **more** charming   **most** charming
cheerful   **more** cheerful   **most** cheerful
comfortable   **more** comfortable   **most** comfortable
delicious   **more** delicious   **most** delicious

Adjectives that form their comparative and superlative with **more** and **most** are usually adjectives with two or more **syllables**, or sounds. For example:

ac-tive   ex-pen-sive
beau-ti-ful   fa-mous
charm-ing   for-tu-nate
cheer-ful   in-tel-li-gent
com-fort-a-ble   pow-er-ful
de-li-cious   val-u-a-ble

The comparative and superlative forms of some adjectives are completely different words.

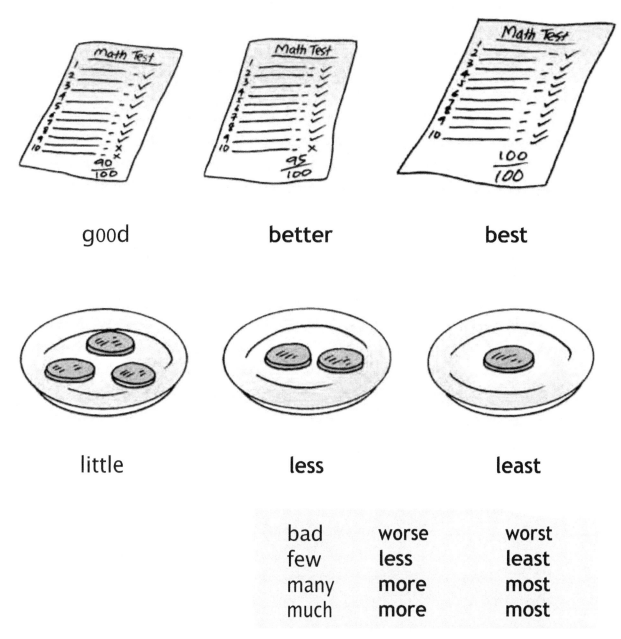

good	better	best

little	less	least

bad	worse	worst
few	less	least
many	more	most
much	more	most

Grammar Help

With these adjectives, you don't add **-er** or **more** to form the comparative, or **-est** or **most** to form the superlative.

Exercise 1

Fill in the blanks with the correct *comparative* and *superlative* forms of the following *adjectives*.

	Comparative	Superlative
hard	_____	_____
cold	_____	_____
soft	_____	_____
tall	_____	_____
rich	_____	_____
mad	_____	_____
funny	_____	_____
big	_____	_____
sad	_____	_____
busy	_____	_____
noisy	_____	_____

Exercise 2

Fill in the blanks with the correct *comparative* and *superlative* forms of the following *adjectives*.

	Comparative	Superlative
foolish	_____	_____
harmful	_____	_____
poisonous	_____	_____
valuable	_____	_____
difficult	_____	_____
generous	_____	_____

6 Determiners

> **Determiners** are words such as **this, those, my, their, which.** They are special adjectives that are used before nouns.

The Articles

> The words **a, an** and **the** belong to this group of words called **determiners.**
>
> The words **a** and **an** are called **indefinite articles.** You can use them with singular nouns to talk about any single person or thing.

Can you hear **a** bird singing ?

Do you wear **a** uniform to school?

This is a picture of an elephant.
Rudy is reading a book.
Mom bought me a new dress today.
You will need an umbrella when you go out.
She eats an apple a day.

Grammar Help

> The article **an** is usually used before words beginning with **vowels.** The article **a** is used before words beginning with **consonants.**

The word **the** is called the **definite article**. Use **the** before a noun when you are talking about a certain person or thing.

The telephone is ringing.

Tom has won **the** race.

Where's **the** cat?
I think she is under **the** bed.

Granny is sitting in **the** garden.
The street is very busy today.
The sky is getting dark.

The ice is melting.

Grammar Help

You also use **the** before a noun when there is only **one**. For example:

the sun
the moon
the sky
the front door of my house

Demonstrative Determiners

The words **this**, **that**, **these** and **those** are determiners. They are used to tell which thing or person you mean. These words are called **demonstrative determiners**, or **demonstrative adjectives**.

I am keeping **these** books.
I am selling **those** books.

James lives in **this** house.

This ice cream is delicious.
How much is t**hat** racket?
What is **that** animal?
Bring me **that** ball.
Would you like **these** apples?

You use **this** and **these** to point to people or things **near** you.

You use **that** and **those** to point to people or things that are **farther** from you.

You use **this** and **that** before singular nouns.
You use **these** and **those** before plural nouns.

Here's a table to help you remember the rules:

Singular	Plural
this	these
that	those

Interrogative Determiners

Use the words **what**, **which** and **whose** before nouns to ask about people or things. These words are called **interrogative determiners** or **interrrogative adjectives**.

What size do you wear?

What kind of bird is that?

What time is it?

What color is her hair?

What kind of clothes do you like to wear?

Which school do you go to?

Which doll is your favorite?

Which road leads to the zoo?

Which runner is the winner?

Do you know **which** girl won the prize?

Whose footprints are these?

Whose baby is this?

Whose dog was barking in the middle of the night?

Possessive Determiners

The words **my**, **your**, **his**, **her**, **its**, **our**, **their** are called **possessive determiners** or **posessive adjectives**. Use these words before nouns to say who something belongs to.

I lent Margaret **my** guitar.

Is this **your** house?

Robert, **your** handwriting is difficult to read.

Michael is showing **his** tortoise to **his** friends.

My sister lost **her** way in the city.

The lion is chasing **its** prey.

The dentist asked **his** patient to open **her** mouth.

Grammar Help

Here is a table to help you remember the **possessive determiners**.

	Singular	Plural
First person	my	our
Second person	your	your
Third person	his	their
	her	their
	its	their

Exercise 1
Fill in the blanks with _a_, _an_ or _the_.

1 _____ owl   7 _____ moon

2 _____ rocket   8 _____ Missouri River

3 _____ apron   9 _____ mango

4 _____ sun   10 _____ animal

5 _____ page   11 _____ eagle

6 _____ computer   12 _____ baby

Exercise 2
Write _a_, _an_ or _the_ in the blanks to complete the sentences.

1 There is _____ rainbow in _____ sky.

2 Who is _____ man outside _____ gate?

3 _____ doctor gave Jane _____ injection.

4 Paul opened _____ door to let _____ dog in.

5 Mark is _____ only child in _____ family.

6 What's _____ largest animal in _____ world?

7 There's _____ nest in _____ tree.

8 Sue is writing _____ letter to her grandfather.

9 Jack has _____ brother and _____ sister.

10 We reached _____ top of _____ hill in two hours.

Exercise 3

Fill in the blanks with the correct *demonstrative adjectives*.

1 Come and look at _____ insects.

2 Stop _____ man!

3 I was in fifth grade last year. I am in sixth grade _____ year.

4 Bring _____ chairs here.

5 _____ ice cream is delicious.

6 Can you see _____ stars in the sky?

Exercise 4

Are the underlined words *demonstrative adjectives* or *demonstrative pronouns*? Write *DA* (for demonstrative adjectives) or *DP* (for demonstrative pronouns) in the blanks.

1 <u>This</u> house has five bedrooms.   _____

2 Who is <u>that</u> man?   _____

3 <u>This</u> is our school.   _____

4 <u>These</u> are wild animals.   _____

5 <u>That</u> is right.   _____

6 What's <u>that</u> noise?   _____

7 <u>These</u> books are Jane's.   _____

8 <u>Those</u> books belong to me.   _____

9 <u>These</u> are donkeys.   _____

10 <u>Those</u> are horses.   _____

Exercise 5

Choose the correct *possessive adjectives* from the box to fill in the blanks.

my	his	your	her
its	our	their	

1   Is this Jane's dog? Yes, this is _____ dog.

2   The dog is chasing _____ own tail.

3   Peter, is _____ father at home?

4   Rudy is showing _____ stamps to Ali.

5   I am going to _____ aunt's house this evening.

6   We always keep _____ classroom clean.

7   Children, have you all finished _____ homework?

8   The children are proud of _____ school.

Exercise 6

Choose the correct *interrogative adjectives* from the box to fill in the blanks.

what	which	whose

1   _____ kind of animal is that?

2   _____ runner is the winner?

3   _____ is the matter?

4   _____ desk is this?

5   _____ handphone is ringing?

6   _____ is your name?

7   _____ twin is taller?

8   _____ hand is holding the pebble?

Verbs and Tenses

Most **verbs** are **action words**. They tell you what people, animals or things are doing.

knock

burst

climb

dig

read

drop

Word File

act	jump
bake	move
bend	pull
buy	run
close	shout
cook	sing
cross	sit
fall	slide
fly	stand
go	start
grow	swim
hop	walk

The Simple Present Tense

> The **simple present tense** expresses a general truth or a customary action.

Uncle Joe **wears** glasses.

The sun **rises** in the east.

Ducks **love** water.

The children **go** to school by bus.

Mary **enjoys** singing.

Peter sometimes **lends** me his bike.

Cows **eat** grass.

Monkeys **like** bananas.

Tom **collects** stamps.

The earth **goes** around the sun.

It often **snows** in winter.

We always **wash** our hands before meals.

We **eat** three meals a day.

Father **takes** the dog for a walk every morning.

Use the simple present tense to talk about things that are planned for the future.

Melanie **starts** school tomorrow.

Next week I **go** to summer camp.

The train **departs** in five minutes.

We **join** the senior scout troop in July this year. My big brother **leaves** school at 4 o'clock.

The new supermarket **opens** next Friday.

The new grammar book **comes** out in September.

Grandad **retires** next year.

We **fly** to London next Thursday.

The plane **lands** at 5:30 P.M.

We **move** to our new house in a month.

My big sister **begins** her summer job next week.

Exercise 1

Underline the *verbs* in the following sentences.

1 The children go to school by bus.

2 Bats sleep during the day.

3 These toys belong to Kathy.

4 Every pupil has a good dictionary.

5 Polar bears live at the North Pole.

6 Most children learn very fast.

7 Mr. Thomas teaches us science.

8 The earth goes around the sun.

9 We never cross the street without looking.

10 Many stores close on Sunday.

Exercise 2

Fill in the blanks with the *simple present tense* of the verbs in parentheses.

1 Winter _____ after autumn. (come)

2 A dog _____. (bark)

3 You _____ tired. (look)

4 Everyone _____ mistakes. (make)

5 Ali _____ in a department store. (work)

6 Judy _____ English very well. (speak)

7 Tim's knee _____. (hurt)

8 Monkeys _____ bananas. (like)

9 Kate always _____ sandwiches for lunch. (eat)

10 He _____ very fast. (type)

Am, Is and Are

The words **am**, **is**, **are** are also verbs, but they are not action words. They are the simple present tense of the verb **be.**

Use **am** with the pronoun **I**, and **is** with the pronouns **he**, **she** and **it**. Use **are** with the pronouns **you**, **we** and **they**.

It **is** a donkey.
It **is** not a horse.

It **is** very hot today.
It **is** not very comfortable.

the verb 'be'

am   is   are

I **am** Peter. I **am** not Paul.

She **is** Miss Lee. She **is** a teacher.

He **is** my father. He **is** a doctor. He **is** not a lawyer. You **are** a stranger. You **are** not my friend.

We **are** in the same class, but we **are** not on the same team.

They **are** good friends. They **are** not enemies.

Here's a table to help you remember how to use **am, is** and **are**:

	Singular	Plural
First person	I am	we are
Second person	you are	you are
Third person	he is	they are
	she is	they are
	it is	they are

Learn these short forms called contractions:

I am	=	I'm	they are	=	they're
you are	=	you're	we are	=	we're
he is	=	he's			
she is	=	she's			
it is	=	it's			
am not	=	aren't (only in questions)			
is not	=	isn't			
are not	=	aren't			

In questions, use **aren't** as a contraction of **am not**. For example, you can say:

> I'm taller than you, **aren't** I?

But in a statement you say:

> I'm **not** as old as you.

Use the verb **is** with singular nouns and **are** with plural nouns.

The camel **is** a desert animal.

Vegetables and fruit **are** healthy foods.

Lambs **are** baby sheep.

Kenneth **is** a lawyer.

Rex **is** a clever dog.

A duck **is** a kind of bird.

The playground **is** full of people today.

My house **is** near the school.

These questions **are** too difficult.

The balloons **are** very colorful.

Those people **are** very busy.

Dad and Mom **are** in the kitchen.

Use **is** and **are** with the word **there** to say what you can see and hear.

There is a castle on the hill.
There are some clouds in the sky.

There is a wasps' nest
  in the tree.

There is a fence around the school.

There are a lot of books in the library.

There are two guards at the gate.

Is there any food in the fridge?

Are there any apples left on the tree?

How much rice **is there**?

There are a few sharks in the bay.

There are enough candies for everyone, **aren't there**?

There are two pigeons on the roof.

Grammar Help

Learn this contraction:

there is   =   there's

Exercise 1

Fill in the blanks with *am*, *is* or *are*.

1 They _____ my good friends.

2 He _____ a soldier.

3 You _____ taller than Charlie.

4 She _____ ill.

5 We _____ very hungry.

6 It _____ a sunny day.

7 I _____ angry with Joe.

8 You _____ all welcome to my house.

Exercise 2

Fill in the blanks with *is* or *are*.

1 John's dog _____ very friendly.

2 Robert _____ ten years old.

3 These flowers _____ very pretty.

4 The two schools _____ close to each other.

5 Math _____ not a very difficult subject.

6 _____ dinner ready?

7 This computer _____ very easy to use.

8 All the windows _____ open.

9 Sue and Jane _____ neighbors.

10 His hair _____ curly.

Exercise 3

Fill in the blanks with *There is* or *There are*.

1 _____ a fence around the barn.

2 _____ trees along the road.

3 _____ a rainbow in the sky.

4 _____ lots of parks in our town.

5 _____ nothing in the cupboard.

6 _____ not many bedrooms in the new house.

7 _____ lots of mistakes on your test paper.

8 _____ a wasps' nest in the tree.

9 _____ ants in the cookies.

10 _____ many different kinds of animals
in the zoo.

11 _____ plenty of food on the table.

12 _____ a church on the hilltop.

13 _____ no more water in the pool.

14 _____ too many people on the beach.

15 _____ only a few customers in the shop.

The Present Progressive Tense

When do you use the **present progressive tense**? To talk about actions in the present, or things that are still going on or happening now.

Mom is **knitting** a sweater for Sally.

I **am writing** a letter.

The phone **is ringing**.

I'**m playing** chess with my friend.

She'**s riding** a horse.

He'**s taking** a walk in the park.

The man'**s counting** the money.

They **are practicing** tai chi.

We'**re rushing** to the airport to meet Mr. Smith.

They **are still sleeping**.

They **are swimming** in the sea.

What **are** they **doing**?

What'**s happening**?

Why **aren't** you **doing** your homework?

Aren't I sitting up straight?

4 Form the present progressive tense like this:

  am + present participle
  is + present participle
  are + present participle

4 The **present participle** is the form of a verb ending with -**ing**. For example:

  show + ing =   showing
  come + ing =   coming

4 You have to double the last letter of some verbs before you add -**ing**. For example:

  get + ing = ge**tt**ing   rob + ing = ro**bb**ing
  nod + ing = no**dd**ing   stop + ing = sto**pp**ing
  jog + ing = jo**gg**ing   swim + ing = swi**mm**ing

4 Notice that the verbs above are all **short verbs** of just **one syllable**.

  They all end with a **consonant** such as **b, d, g, m, p, t** and have only **one vowel** before the consonant.

4 If a verb ends in **e**, you usually have to drop the **e** before you add -**ing**. For example:

  chase + ing =   chasing
  cycle + ing =   cycling
  drive + ing =   driving
  smile + ing =   smiling

Use the present progressive tense to talk about things you have planned to do, or things that are going to happen in the future. To form the present progressive tense, use **am**, **is** and **are** as **helping verbs** or **auxiliary verbs**.

When **are** you **taking**
me to the zoo?

We **are having** a barbecue
later this evening.

We **are going** camping tomorrow.

I'**m starting** piano lessons soon.

Jim's parents **are taking** him to Texas next week.

My favorite TV program **is starting** in a minute.

All our friends **are coming**.

Who'**s bringing** salad for the barbecue? I **am**.

I **am visiting** Joe next week.

Where **are** you **going** for your vacation? What

are we **eating** for dinner?

Exercise 1

Write the *present participle* of these verbs on the blanks.

1 come _____
2 run _____
3 sleep _____
4 fall _____
5 jump _____
6 climb _____

7 go _____
8 ask _____
9 catch _____
10 write _____
11 drop _____
12 bring _____

Exercise 2

Fill in the blanks with the *present progressive tense* of the verbs in parentheses.

1 They _____ the roller-coaster ride. (enjoy)

2 Jill _____ her hair. (wash)

3 It _____ dark. (get)

4 The dentist _____ Sue's teeth. (examine)

5 The train _____ through the tunnel. (pass)

6 The men _____ very hard in the sun. (work)

7 What _____ the theater _____ today? (show)

8 We _____ a snowman. (make)

9 The plane _____ above the clouds. (fly)

10 The teachers _____ a meeting. (have)

Have and Has

The verbs **have** and **has** are used to say what people own or possess. They are also used to talk about things that people do or get, such as illnesses. These words are the simple present tense of the verb **have**.

Peter **has** a sore knee.

We **have** breakfast at 7:00 A.M.

He **has** a lot of stamps.

She **has** long hair.

our house **has** large windows. I

have a younger brother.

We **have** art lessons on Mondays.

Have a cookie, if you like.

Dad **has** a cold.

Jenny often **has** sandwiches for lunch.

Monkeys **have** long tails.

Use **has** with **he, she, it**, and with **singular nouns**. Use **have** with **I, you, we, they**, and with **plural nouns**.

Here is a table to help you remember the rules:

	Singular	Plural
First person	I have	we have
Second person	you have	you have
Third person	he has	they have
	she has	they have
	it has	they have

Learn these contractions:

I have	=	I've
you have	=	you've
he has	=	he's
she has	=	she's
it has	=	it's
we have	=	we've
they have	=	they've
have not	=	haven't
has not	=	hasn't

Exercise 1

Fill in the blanks with *have* or *has*.

1 We _____ a new science teacher.

2 He _____ a bad temper.

3 I often _____ fruit for dessert.

4 You _____ a good chance of winning the prize.

5 She always _____ oatmeal for breakfast.

6 The broom _____ a blue handle.

7 They never _____ any problem with tests.

Exercise 2

Fill in the blanks with *have* or *has*.

1 The girls _____ golden hair.

2 An insect _____ six legs.

3 Dad _____ his cell phone with him.

4 The children _____ a new swing set.

5 Many poor people _____ nothing to eat.

6 Chicago _____ a very big airport.

7 A triangle _____ three sides.

8 The man _____ two daughters.

9 James _____ a toothache.

10 All the passengers _____ their tickets.

The Present Perfect Tense

Use the **present perfect tense** to talk about happenings in the past that explain or affect the present. The verbs **have** and **has** are used as "helping" or auxiliary verbs to form the present perfect tense.

It's **been** very wet today.

Kim's **cut** her finger.

Sam **has scored** two goals.

I've just **finished** my shower.

Uncle Tom **has lost** his wallet.

John **has gone** out.

The Lees **have moved** to Ohio.

It **has not rained** for months.

Have you **found** your keys yet?

Tim **has made** two spelling mistakes.

They **have opened** a new shop.

Grammar Help

To form the **present perfect tense** join **have** or **has** to the past participle of the verb:

> have + past participle
> has + past participle

The **past participle** of a regular verb usually ends in **-ed**, just like the simple past tense. But the past participles of irregular verbs don't follow this rule.

Exercise 1
Write the *past participle* of these verbs on the blanks.

1 break _____   6 buy _____

2 drink _____   7 find _____

3 cut _____   8 draw _____

4 do _____   9 hear _____

5 sing _____   10 know _____

Exercise 2
Fill in the blanks with the *present perfect tense* of the verbs in parentheses.

1 Dad _____ his car key. (lose)

2 All the guests _____. (arrive)

3 Tony _____ a goal. (score)

4 Peter _____ in the tent several times. (sleep)

5 It _____ not _____ for two months. (rain)

6 Some prisoners _____ from the prison. (escape)

7 The plane _____ at the airport. (land)

8 John _____ a puppet. (make)

9 Dad and I _____ a big fish. (catch)

10 I _____ this movie twice. (see)

The Simple Past Tense

Use the **simple past tense** to talk about things that happened in the past. The simple past tense is also used to talk about things that happened in stories.

The wicked Queen **gave** Snow White a poisoned apple.

Pinocchio's nose **grew** longer every time he told a lie.

Dinosaurs **lived** millions of years ago.

I **bought** a new camera last week.

Joe **learned** to play the guitar very quickly.

We **drove** to the safari park last weekend.

The giant panda **gave** birth to a cub last night.

Yesterday Dad **took** me to the carnival.

The plane **landed** a few minutes ago.

The children **visited** a farm during the holidays.

Who **invented** the computer?

Jack and Jill **went** up the hill.

Little Red Riding Hood **decided** to visit her grandmother.

The Three Bears **found** Goldilocks asleep in their house.

Regular and Irregular Verbs

> The simple past tense of most verbs ends in -**ed**. These verbs are called **regular verbs**.

Spelling File

Base Form	Simple Past
aim	aimed
bake	baked
open	opened
happen	happened
pull	pulled
push	pushed
scold	scolded
shout	shouted
visit	visited
wait	waited
walk	walked
work	worked

Who **closed** all
the windows?

It **snowed** last night.

Mom **opened** the door for us.

Sally **petted** the dog.

That event **happened** long ago.

We **visited** our uncle last week.

They **walked** to school together yesterday. They

worked until twelve last night.

Dad **tried** to fix the light.

William Tell **aimed** at the apple on his son's head.

4 The **simple past tense** is usually formed by adding -**ed** to the verb. For example:

jump + ed = jumped   lift + ed = lifted
laugh + ed = laughed   look + ed = looked

4 If the verb ends with -**e**, just add -**d**. For example:

agree + d = agreed   hate + d = hated
die + d = died   live + d = lived

4 Remember these spelling rules:
You must double the last letter of some verbs before adding -**ed**. For example:

fan + ed = fan**n**ed   pat + ed = pat**t**ed
grab + ed = grab**b**ed   rip + ed = rip**p**ed
nod + ed = nod**d**ed   slam + ed = slam**m**ed

4 Notice that the verbs above are all **short verbs** of just **one syllable**. They all end with a **consonant** such as **b, d, m, n, p, t**, and have only a **single vowel** before the consonant.

4 With verbs that end in -**y**, change the **y** to **i** before adding -**ed**. For example:

bury + ed = buried   fry + ed = fried
carry + ed = carried   hurry + ed = hurried
cry + ed = cried   try + ed = tried

The simple past form of some verbs does *not* end in -**ed**. Such verbs are called **irregular verbs**.

The simple past tense of some irregular verbs does *not* change at all.

David **hurt** his foot when he jumped over the drain.

The worker **cut** down the tree this morning.

Her ring **cost** only 10 dollars.

He **hit** the ball over the net.

Dad **read** to us last night.

He **shut** the door.

I **put** some sugar in my coffee.

Spelling File	
Base Form	Simple Past
beat	beat
burst	burst
cost	cost
cut	cut
hit	hit
hurt	hurt
put	put
read	read
split	split
shut	shut

Most irregular verbs, however, take a different form in the simple past tense.

Sam **bent** the stick in two.

Spelling File

Base Form	Simple Past
bend	bent
break	broke
bring	brought
buy	bought
fall	fell
fly	flew
get	got
hear	heard
keep	kept
lose	lost
sell	sold
shoot	shot
sleep	slept

Tom **shot** and scored a goal.

I **lost** my pen on the bus.
We **sold** our car last week.
The baby **slept** right thought the night.
Peter **got** a watch for his birthday.
I **heard** a noise in the night.
He **brought** his pet mouse to school. My
book **fell** off the desk.

A bird **flew** into
the classroom.

Exercise 1

Write the *simple past tense* of these verbs on the blanks.

1	take	_____	7	tell	_____
2	walk	_____	8	write	_____
3	rain	_____	9	sit	_____
4	shut	_____	10	read	_____
5	open	_____	11	close	_____
6	cry	_____	12	cook	_____

Exercise 2

Fill in the blanks with the correct *simple past tense* of the verbs in parentheses.

1 She _____ home alone. (go)

2 The wind _____ throughout the night. (blow)

3 An apple _____ on his head. (drop)

4 The Princess's ball _____ into the well. (roll)

5 A frog _____ into the well and _____ it back to her. (jump/bring)

6 Jack _____ the highest grade in his English class. (get)

7 The party _____ at 8:00 P.M. (begin)

8 He _____ his old car and _____ a new one. (sell/buy)

9 Jack _____ up the ladder carefully. (climb)

10 Who _____ all the windows? (shut)

Was and Were

The verbs **was** and **were** are also forms of the verb **be**. **Was** is the simple past tense of **am** and **is**. Use **was** with the pronouns **I**, **he**, **she** and **it**, and with **singular nouns**.

Edison **was** a famous inventor.

Beethoven **was** a German composer.
Sue **was** at the library this morning.
It **was** very wet on Monday.
Ten years ago she **was** only a baby.
He **was** not well yesterday.
Last year she **wasn't** tall enough to reach the high shelf.
Samantha **was** second in the race, **wasn't she**?

Were is the simple past tense of **are**. Use **were** with the pronouns **you**, **we** and **they**, and with plural nouns.

These **were** my best jeans.

The Romans **were** brave soldiers.
They **were** third in the wheelbarrow race.
There **weren't** any clouds in the sky.
Were you still in bed when I phoned?
We **were** on the same school team.
Those **were** my best jeans.

Here is a table to help you remember the rules:

	Singular	Plural
First person	I was	we were
Second person	you were	you were
Third person	he was	they were
	she was	they were
	it was	they were

Here's a table to show you the different forms of the verb **be**:

	Simple Present	Simple Past
First person singular	am	was
Second person singular	are	were
Third person singular	is	was
First person plural	are	were
Second person plural	are	were
Third person plural	are	were

Learn these contractions:

was not = wasn't
were not = weren't

The Past Progressive Tense

Use the **past progressive tense** to talk about actions that were going on at a certain moment in the past.

Mary **was waiting** for the bus when Peter passed by.

Miss May **was cleaning** the chalkboard.
Sally **was packing** her books into her schoolbag.
Jenny and I **were tidying** the classroom.
The twins **were fighting** in the corner.
Michael and John **were washing** the paint brushes.
Mom **was cooking** our supper when I came home.

Grammar Help

You form the **past progressive tense** like this:

was + present participle
were + present participle

In the examples above, **was** and **were** are called **helping verbs,** or **auxiliary verbs.** They help to form the **past progressive tense** when you join them to the **present participle** (the form of verbs ending in **-ing**) . For example:

Ben **was doing** his homework.
Peter **was making** a model of a bridge.

Exercise 1

Fill in the blanks with *was* or *were*.

1 We _____ the champions last year.

2 Where is James? He _____ here just now.

3 Mom and Dad _____ on vacation last week.

4 The weather _____ fine this morning.

5 There _____ a lot of people at our party yesterday.

6 There _____ a small lake here many years ago.

7 He _____ sick yesterday.

8 Don't blame him. It _____ my mistake.

Exercise 2

When Miss May walked into the class what were the children doing? Fill in the blanks with the correct *past progressive tense* of the verbs in brackets.

1 James _____ to Peter. (talk)

2 Sue _____ a storybook. (read)

3 Rudy _____ the chalkboard. (erase)

4 David _____ his math exercise. (do)

5 Peter _____ Joe his new watch. (show)

6 Jane _____ a horse in her notebook. (draw)

7 Ahmad _____ for his pencil. (look)

8 Some children _____ a lot of noise. (make)

The Future Tense

Use the **future tense** for things that have not happened yet, but are going to happen.

Use the verbs **shall** and **will** as **helping verbs** or **auxiliary verbs** to form the future tense.

I **shall be** eight years old
next year.

They **will finish** the job
next week.

The weatherman
says it **will rain**
this afternoon.

We **shall play** a game of chess after lunch.

You **will be** sick if you eat too much.

I hope it **won't rain** tomorrow.

Sharon is ill. She **will not be** at the party.

You **will enjoy** visiting New Zealand.

Dad **will be** back for dinner.

He **will make** lots of friends at his new school.

Use **shall** or **will** with **I** and **we**.
Use **will** with **you, he, she, it** and **they**.

Here is a table to help you remember the rules:

	Singular	Plural
First person	I shall	we shall
	I will	we will
Second person	you will	you will
Third person	he will	they will
	she will	they will
	it will	they will

Learn these contractions:

I shall	= I'll	we shall	= we'll
I will	= I'll	we will	= we'll
you will	= you'll	they will	= they'll
he will	= he'll		
she will	= she'll	shall not	= shan't
it will	= it'll	will not	= won't

I
we
shall/will

you
he
she
it
will

There are other ways of talking about future actions and happenings.

You can use **going to**.

I think I'm **going to be** sick.

We **are going to bake** a cake this afternoon.

I'm sure Mom and Dad **are going to be** proud of me.

When **are** you **going to clean** your room?

They **are going to wash** the car for Dad.

It **is going to get** dark very soon.

You can also use the **simple present tense** to talk about things that have been arranged for the future.

The new supermarket **opens** tomorrow.

James **moves** to the second grade next year.

The new school year **starts** on Monday.

Next month I **go** to summer camp.

We **have** a history test next week.

The bus **leaves** in ten minutes.

Exercise 1

Fill in the blanks with the correct *future tense* of the verbs in brackets, using *shall* or *will*.

1 You _____ fat if you eat too many desserts. (grow)

2 The new school building _____ ready soon. (be)

3 We _____ to the zoo after breakfast. (go)

4 I _____ my bath before dinner. (take)

5 Peter _____ lots to do on his grandmother's farm. (find)

6 If we ask her, she _____ us how to play chess. (teach)

7 If he works hard, he _____ his exams. (pass)

8 _____ we _____ home now? (go)

Exercise 2

Complete these sentences by changing *shall* or *will* to the appropriate form of the verb *be* + *going to* (i.e., *am*, *is*, or *are* + *going to*).

1 They will be busy tomorrow.
   They _____ be busy tomorrow.

2 I hope I will be ready on time.
   I hope I _____ be ready on time.

3 We shall visit James this evening.
   We _____ visit James this evening.

4 It will rain soon.
   It _____ rain soon.

5 Dad will take us to the movies tomorrow.
   Dad _____ take us to the movies tomorrow.

Can and Could

The verbs **can** and **could** are both **helping** or **auxiliary verbs.** Use **can** and **could** to talk about people's **ability** to do things.

Can and **could** are used with the pronouns **I, you, he, she, it, we** and **they,** and with **singular** or **plural nouns.**

Could is the past tense of **can.**

Jack ran as far as he **could.**

Some birds **cannot fly.**

He **can run** faster than Arthur.

She **cannot afford** such an expensive ring.

I'm full. I **can't eat** any more.

Can you **help** me?

Can I **come** with you?

I knew you **could do** it if you tried.

She **could not come** because she was ill.

Miss Lee said we **could go** home early.

All the King's men **could not put** Humpty Dumpty together again.

May and Might

May and **might** are **helping** or **auxiliary verbs,** too.

4 Use **may** to ask if you are allowed to do something, or to give someone permission to do something.

May I watch television now? Yes, you **may**.

May I borrow your pen?

You **may come** in.

You **may go** now.

4 **May** is also used to talk about things that are likely to happen.

Take an umbrella. It **may rain**.

If it continues to rain, there **may be** a flood.

I **may go** to Sue's birthday party if I'm free.

You **may fall** down if you aren't careful.

4 **Might** is used as the past tense of **may**.

He realized he **might catch** the earlier train if he hurried.
I knew my teacher **might find** out.

Grammar Help

You can also use **might** to talk about things that are possible. For example:

Put your purse away or it **might get** stolen. You **might slip**, so hold on to the railing.

Exercise

Fill in the blanks with *can*, *could*, *may* or *might*.

1 _____ you jump over the hurdle?

2 We ran as fast as we _____.

3 Some people _____ speak three languages.

4 Jean _____ dance quite well.

5 The man is shouting. He _____ need help.

6 If you hurry you _____ catch the train.

7 Dave doesn't look well. He _____ have a fever.

8 The baby is crying. She _____ be hungry.

9 _____ I borrow your bike?

10 I don't know where Jane is. You _____ find her in the library.

11 _____ you drive?

12 Who _____ answer the question?

13 _____ you show me the way to the zoo?

14 He _____ play the piano.

Do, Does and Did

Use **do**, **does** and **did** to talk about actions.

Use **do** with the pronouns **I**, **you**, **we** and **they**, and with **plural nouns**. Use **does** with the pronouns **he**, **she** and **it**, and **singular nouns**.

Did is the **simple past tense** of **do** and **does**.

Dad **does** the dishes.

Mom **does** the cooking.

We always **do** exercise together.

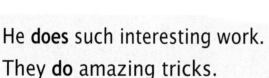

He **does** such interesting work.
They **do** amazing tricks.

Who **did** this drawing?
Henry **did**.

Sally **did** her hair in front of the mirror.

They **did** the dusting and cleaning.

Jane **did** all the laundry by herself.

You **did** well in the test.

I **did** poorly on my exam.

4 Here's a table to remind you about the use of
   do and **does**:

	Singular	Plural
First person	I do	we do
Second person	you do	you do
Third person	he does	they do
	she does	they do
	it does	they do

4 Here's a table to remind you about the use of
   the verb **did**:

	Singular	Plural
First person	I did	we did
Second person	you did	you did
Third person	he did	they did
	she did	they did
	it did	they did

4 Learn these contractions:

do not	=	don't
does not	=	doesn't
did not	=	didn't

You can also use **do**, **does** and **did** as **helping verbs** to ask and answer questions.

Where **did** you find
the wallet?

Do ducks **like** water?
Yes, they **do**.

Do you **like** ice cream? Yes, I **do**.

Does it **rain** often here? Yes, it **does**.

Does he **enjoy** music? Yes, he **does**.

Did it **snow** last night? No, it **didn't**.

Who wants to come with me to the zoo? We all **do**!

What **do** you **want** for lunch?

Who broke this vase? Peter **did**!

Does Ken often **come** home late? Yes, he **does**.

Why **did** he **leave** so suddenly?

Does everyone **have** a dictionary?

Use **do not**, **does not** and **did not** to make other verbs **negative**.

The baby **does not look** very happy.

Dad **did not catch** his train.

The garden looks lovely, **doesn't** it? Yes, it **does**.

Cats **do not** like water.

I **don't enjoy** difficult math tests.

Sophie **doesn't want** to go to school.

He **didn't get** to the station in time.

Don't you **have** a ticket? No, I **don't**.

Don't they **go** to the gym on Mondays? Yes, they **do**.

Didn't they **win**? No, they **didn't**.

You **didn't draw** that picture yourself, **did** you?

Did you **see** the rainbow? No, I **didn't**.

Do not forget to switch off the air conditioner.

Don't tell lies!

Exercise

Fill in the blanks with *do*, *does* or *did*.

1 The shoes were too small. They _____ not fit me.

2 Jack _____ not do well on the exam last week.

3 Where _____ eggs come from?

4 The vase is broken. Who _____ that?

5 What _____ this word mean?

6 How _____ the computer work?

7 _____ he drink coffee?

8 Who _____ that drawing?

9 Where _____ you buy that dress?

10 How _____ you spell your name?

11 _____ not play on a busy street!

12 _____ your work quietly!

13 _____ a snake have legs?

14 He _____ not have any brothers.

15 _____ cats like to eat fish?

Would and Should

The verb **would** is another **helping** or **auxiliary verb**.
Use **would** as the past tense of **will**.

We started running so we
would get there in time.

Peter said he **would come**.
I knew you **would enjoy** Disneyland.
The Prince said he **would** only
marry a true princess.
John and Sue said they
would meet me at the airport.
He promised he **wouldn't forget**
her birthday.

Grammar Help

It is polite to use **would like** when you are
offering people things, or asking for something
yourself. For example:

Would you **like** a cup of coffee?
I am tired now. I'**d like** a rest.
You'**d like** a meal now, **wouldn't** you?
What color **would** you **like**?

Did you know?

When they are accepting an offer, people
often use **would love** instead of **would like**.
For example:

Would you **like** a chocolate?
Yes, please, I **would love** one.

Should is a **helping** or **auxiliary verb.** Use **should** to talk about necessary actions or things that people ought to do.

Children **should not play** in traffic.

You **should** always **look** before crossing the street.

If you are tired you **should go** to bed early.

You **should know** how to spell your own name. We **should** all **drink** more water.

You **should do** more exercise.

Should I **turn** off the computer when I'm not using it?

Shouldn't you **tell** your Mom if you're going out?

We **should** always thank people for presents, **shouldn't** we?

Grammar Help

Learn these contractions:

I would	= I'd	we would	= we'd
you would	= you'd	they would	= they'd
he would	= he'd	should not	= shouldn't
she would	= she'd	would not	= wouldn't

Exercise

Fill in the blanks with *would* or *should*.

1 Every student _____ have a good dictionary.

2 _____ you like some coffee?

3 Yes, I _____ love a cup of coffee.

4 We _____ all learn good table manners.

5 We _____ like to go outdoors if it stops raining. help

6 John said he _____ me with science.

7 _____ you like to play a game with me?

8 Children _____ not watch too much television.

9 You _____ not play with fire.

10 He promised he _____ meet me after school.

11 We _____ not waste water.

12 You _____ all pay attention in class.

13 What _____ we do now?

14 _____ you help if I asked?

15 of course, I _____ help you!

8 Subject-Verb Agreement

When you write a sentence you must make sure that the **subject** and the **verb** agree.

If the subject is a **singular noun**, or the pronoun **he**, **she** or **it**, you need a **singular verb**.

She **enjoys** music.

She **shares** her books with her friends.

The zookeeper **is feeding** the animals.

The children **are playing** on the swings.

The earth **moves** round the sun.

Dad always **drives** to work.

The clerk **is wrapping** a package.

Does everyone **know** the answer?

Mom **has bought** a dress for Sara.

It **is snowing**.

Use a **plural verb** if the subject is a **plural noun**, or the pronoun **we**, **you** or **they**.

The two girls always **walk** home together.

All birds **lay** eggs.

The children are **playing** on the swing.

The stars **shine** brightly on a clear night.

Mom and Dad **love** us a lot.

Do you all **know** the words?

We **have finished** our game of tennis.

They **have** both **worked** very hard.

Collective nouns may be used with either singular or plural verbs. If the group members are all acting together as one, use a singular verb. If the members of the group are acting as individuals, use a plural verb.

The audience **are laughing**.

The band **is playing**.

Singular
That family has moved to Texas.
The team is coached by Mr. Clark.

Plural
The family were giving their opinions.
The team are sharing new ideas.

Our team **has won**.

Grammar Help

Some plural nouns, such as **people**, **cattle**, **police**, don't end with -s. Always use a **plural verb** with these nouns. For example:

People **like** to be praised.
The cattle **are** in the field.
The police **have caught** the thief.

Exercise 1

Fill in the blanks with verbs that match the subjects. Use the correct form of the *simple present tense* of the verbs in parentheses.

1   I always _____ to school with my brother. (go)

2   Mark always _____ to school with his brother. (go)

3   You _____ the answer. (know)

4   Luis _____ the answer, too. (know)

5   This book _____ very few drawings. (have)

6   These books _____ lots of beautiful drawings. (have)

7   Anne _____ my sister. (be)

8   Pat and Alice _____ good at English. (be)

Exercise 2

Fill in the blanks with verbs that match the subjects. Use the correct form of the *simple present tense* of the verbs in parentheses.

1   A tiger _____. (roar)

2   All birds _____ eggs. (lay)

3   Dad _____ listening to music. (like)

4   Uncle Bob _____ his car every day. (wash)

5   She _____ all the answers. (know)

6   There _____ twelve months in a year. (be)

7   The twins often _____ . (fight)

8   our parents _____ us. (love)

9 Adverbs

An **adverb** is a word that describes a verb. It tells you about an action, or the way something is done.

A lot of adverbs end in **-ly**.

They laughed **loudly**.

The baby is sleeping **soundly**.

The dog is barking **fiercely**.

Alice skated **beautifully**.

The Prince and the Princess lived **happily** ever after.

The birds are singing **sweetly**.

It is raining **heavily**.

The dog and the cat live together **peacefully**.

The soldiers fought **bravely**.

The sun is shining **brightly**.

The old man walked **slowly**.

Spelling File

Adjective	Adverb
beautiful	beautifully
brave	bravely
bright	brightly
fierce	fiercely
happy	happily
heavy	heavily
loud	loudly
peaceful	peacefully
slow	slowly
sound	soundly
sweet	sweetly

Grammar Help

Many adverbs are made by adding **-ly** to adjectives.

Some adverbs describe the way something is done.
They are called **adverbs of manner**.

The driver braked **suddenly**.

The parcel arrived **safely**.

The dog jumped up **playfully**.

Please write **legibly**.

Please speak **clearly**.

Look **closely** at these footprints.

You have all answered **correctly**.

You can shop **cheaply** at this store.

Jamal dressed **smartly** for the party.

Maria is behaving **selfishly**.

The man drove **carelessly**.

The twins liked to dress **differently**.

She played **skillfully**.

Spelling File	
Adjective	Adverb
careless	carelessly
cheap	cheaply
clear	clearly
close	closely
correct	correctly
different	differently
playful	playfully
safe	safely
selfish	selfishly
skillful	skillfully
smart	smartly

Some adverbs describe when something happens.
They are called **adverbs of time**.

Can I do my work **later**?
No, do it **now**.

Paul has **just** arrived.

He **often** swims in the evening.

Lisa is **always** cheerful.

Sometimes I ride my bike to school.

Everyone arrived **early**.

David arrived **late**.

It's snowing **again**.

The mother bird started to build her nest **yesterday**.

She is continuing to build it **today**.

She will finish it **tomorrow**.

John's shoes were too big for him **last year**.

They fit him **this year**.

They will be too small for him **next year**.

It rained **last night**.

The weather is fine **this morning**.

Some adverbs tell you where something happens. They are called **adverbs of place**.

Mom and Dad are watching television **upstairs**.

The children are playing **downstairs**.

It's raining. Let's go **inside**.

Rex, you can stay **outside**.

Come **here**!

Please put the books **there**.

The workers are moving the rubbish **away**.

The miners are working **underground**.

They are going **abroad** to study.

There are trees **everywhere**.

Alice lived **next door**.

Where's Shamika?

Exercise 1

Rewrite the following adjectives as *adverbs*.

1 slow	_____	7 cool	_____
2 beautiful	_____	8 comfortable	_____
3 strong	_____	9 wise	_____
4 tidy	_____	10 quiet	_____
5 brave	_____	11 merry	_____
6 soft	_____	12 busy	_____

Exercise 2

Underline the *adverbs* in the following sentences.

1 The man shouted loudly.

2 He arrived early.

3 The train has already left.

4 He drove carelessly.

5 The students talked noisily.

6 The children are playing outside.

7 Let's go now.

8 Tom spoke politely to his teacher.

9 Have you seen Anne's cat anywhere?

10 Come here!

10 Prepositions

A **preposition** is a word that connects one thing with another, showing how they are related.

Some prepositions tell you about **position** or **place.**

There's a big balloon **in** the sky.

Jane is jumping **into** the pool.

The books fell **off** the shelf.

Dad always keeps his wallet **in** the drawer.

There is a long mirror **on** the wall.

The school is **near** the park.

There is an old castle **on** the hill.

The horse jumped **over** the hurdle.

Grammar Help

A **preposition** is usually followed by a noun or pronoun.

Some prepositions are used to talk about **time**.

Many shops close **on** Sundays.

We watched the World Cup game **until** 2:00 A.M.

The trees lose their leaves **during** winter.

We always wash our hands **before** meals.

Dad gets home **about** six **in** the evening.

We get up **in** the morning.

We go to bed **at** night.

It's always hot **in** summer.

The movie starts **at** two **in** the afternoon.

Autumn begins **in** September.

They were married **in** 1990.

Joe arrived **after** me.

It has not rained at all **for** two weeks.

Breakfast is served **at** seven o'clock.

Kevin and Joe have been in the same class **since** first grade.

Exercise 1

Underline the *prepositions* in the following sentences.

1 The man fell off the ladder.

2 We have dinner at 7:30 P.M.

3 Tom was born on a Friday.

4 There are seven days in a week.

5 Sue is running after her dog.

6 Several people are waiting at the bus stop.

7 I received a letter from Sara yesterday.

8 Why are you still in bed?

Exercise 2

Fill in the blanks with the correct *prepositions* from the box.

near	by	on	at	between
in	around	into	up	behind

1 The bus arrived _____ 8:30 A.M.

2 The children are swimming _____ the pool.

3 There's a picture _____ the wall.

4 There is a fence _____ the house.

5 Granny is sitting _____ fire.

6 Harold is hiding _____ the chair.

7 Jack climbed _____ the beanstalk.

8 We divided the candy _____ us.

9 I dived _____ the river.

10 Don't go too _____ the edge.

11 Conjunctions

A **conjunction** is a linking word such as **and**, **or**, **but**.
Conjunctions are used to connect words or sentences.

The animal is large **but** timid.

Is this a sheep **or** a goat?

a cat **and** its kittens
a builder **and** his tools
a doctor **and** a nurse
slow **but** steady
sweet **or** sour?
a male **or** a female?
A horse, a zebra **or** a donkey?
Paul has a dog, a parrot **and** a cat.

It's cold, wet **and** windy today.

Grammar Help

A **conjunction** may link two or more than two words or sentences.

The words **before, after, as, when, while, until, since,** are also conjunctions. They tell when something happens, so they are called **conjunctions of time**.

Maggie could play the piano **before** she was five.

I always brush my teeth **after** I've had my breakfast.

After he began exercising regularly, Jerry became healthier.

You have grown taller **since** I saw you last.

Look both ways **before** you cross the street.

Joe listened to music **while** he was doing his homework.

Miss Lee was smiling **as** she walked into the class.

Wait here **until** I come back.

Don't leave **until** you've finished your work.

Tran saw an accident **while** he was walking home.

Take all your belongings with you **when** you leave the plane. Joe first met his wife **when** he was studying in London.

Tom and Joe have been friends **since** childhood.

Exercise 1

Complete these sentences with *and*, *but* or *or*.

1 I asked for some bread _____ butter.

2 Mr. _____ Mrs. Chen have three children.

3 Maggie is a good singer _____ a poor dancer.

4 We wish you a Merry Christmas _____ a Happy New Year.

5 Is their new baby a boy _____ a girl?

6 The dictionary has 1000 words _____ 200 drawings.

7 Sue is taller than Nat _____ shorter than Mike.

8 Are you going by train _____ by bus?

Exercise 2

Choose the correct *conjunctions of time* from the box to complete these sentences.

when	while	as	before
after	since	until	

1 Jack always brushes his teeth _____ he has eaten a meal.

2 It started to rain _____ the children were playing in the garden.

3 Let's go home _____ it gets dark.

4 Give this letter to Anne _____ you see her.

5 She has known Jack _____ he was a child.

6 The party began at 8:00 P.M. and lasted _____ midnight.

7 Alice looked unhappy _____ she walked in.

12 Interjections

An **interjection** is a word that expresses a sudden, strong feeling such as **surprise**, **pain**, or **pleasure**.

Cheers!

Oh dear!

Happy Birthday!

Ssh!

Ouch!

Look out!

Wow!
Goodness!
Oh!
Good!
Oh no!
Hooray!
Thanks!
Help!
Good luck!
Well done!
Gosh!
Hey!
Merry Christmas!
Happy New Year!

Did you know?

Notice that an **exclamation point** (!) is often used after interjections.

13 Sentences

What is a Sentence?

A **sentence** is a group of words that expresses a complete thought. A sentence must have a **subject** and a **verb**, but it may or may not have an object.

Subject	Verb	Object
Sally	is making	a doll.
Wendy and Kim	are fighting.	
The hedgehog	curled up.	
Maggie	is reading	a book.
It	is raining.	
Dad	cooked	dinner.
I	am flying	a kite.
We	are eating	our breakfast.
They	are washing	the dishes.
The dentist	is examining	Susan's teeth.
The old couple	have	no children.
Janet	screamed.	

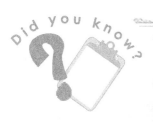

Did you know?

A **sentence** that makes a statement begins with a **capital letter** and ends with a **period**.

Kinds of Sentences

There are **four kinds** of sentences.

4   A **declarative sentence** makes a **statement**.

The children are swimming.

The telephone rang.

Everyone sat down.

Richard is feeding
the hens.

4   An **interrogative sentence** asks a **question**.

Where are the twins?

Are you going shopping today?

What is your name?

What is Richard
doing?

4   An **exclamatory sentence** expresses strong emotion.

What lovely weather!

The silly girl!

How stupid I am!

4   An **imperative sentence** gives an **order**.

Please sit down.

Tell me the truth.

Speak up!

Come back!

The Imperative

Use the base form of a verb to give **commands** or make direct requests. This use of the verb is called the **imperative.**

oK, children, **open** your books to page 25.

Stand, everyone!
Tidy your bedroom immediately!
Choose a partner!
Eat plenty of vegetables.
Find some nice round pebbles.
Come back soon!
Take a sandwich.
Come and **look** at this, Tom!

Imperatives are a very direct way of telling people to do something. Using **do** or **please** before an imperative is more polite.

Please come in.

Do sit down.

Do check these figures again.

Please help yourselves to some food.

Please don't change anything on my computer.

Grammar Help

You can also use the helping verb **would** to sound polite. For example:

Please **would** you clear the table?
Would you please talk quietly?

Exercise

Look at the groups of words below. Do you know which are *sentences* and which are not?

Put a checkmark in the space next to sentences, and an X next to other word groups.

1	Mrs. Chen is a good teacher.	☐
2	not well today	☐
3	Do the work yourself.	☐
4	How are you?	☐
5	basic rules of grammar	☐
6	bread and butter	☐
7	Welcome to the National Zoo.	☐
8	brush his teeth	☐
9	toys in the box	☐
10	more than one	☐
11	What is the time now?	☐
12	Sit down!	☐
13	Please come here.	☐
14	Mark is sleeping.	☐
15	open the door.	☐

The Subject and the Object

The **subject** of a sentence sometimes does something to someone or something else.

The person or thing that receives the action is called the **object**.

Dad is cooking supper.

We have built a sandcastle.

Subject	Verb	Object
Susan	has bought	a painting.
Hannah	is reading	her book.
The twins	climbed	the hill.
James	stroked	the cat.
Mom	is holding	the baby.
Jacob	is making	a kite.
They	were playing	football.
I	am writing	a story.
Emma	crossed	the street.
You	have forgotten	your umbrella.

Direct and Indirect Objects

Some verbs have **two objects**. The **direct object** receives the action of the verb. The **indirect object** tells to whom or for whom the action is done.

Dad bought
James a bike.

Subject	Verb	Indirect Object	Direct Object
The bank	lends	people	money.
Madison	is making	her doll	a dress.
I	am writing	Grandma	a letter.
Grandma	is reading	Diana	a story.
Andrew	gave	his dog	a bone.
We	left	you	some food.
Joshua	is showing	us	his stamps.
Miss Lee	found	Alice	a chair.

The **indirect object** usually comes before the **direct object**.

Exercise 1

Read the following sentences. Then draw a line under the *subjects* and a circle around the *objects*.

1 Anne has drawn a panda.

2 They are playing table tennis.

3 Little Kate knows the alphabet well.

4 Dad bought a computer.

5 I am writing a letter.

6 Birds have feathers.

7 The workmen are building a house.

8 Samantha has a pretty doll.

9 The children received one gift each.

10 Do you know the answer?

Exercise 2

There are two objects in each sentence. Draw a line under the *direct objects* and a circle around the *indirect objects*.

1 Dad gave Dave a present.

2 Mom is making the children a meal.

3 Mr. Thomas bought them ice cream cones.

4 I sent Anne a birthday card.

5 Granny told us a story.

6 The waiter brought the guests their drinks.

7 Can I get you a sandwich?

8 The police officer showed us the way to the museum.

Positive and Negative Sentences

A **positive sentence** tells you that something is so.

A sentence that tells you something is *not* so is called a **negative sentence**. It contains a negative word like **not**, **never**, **no**, **no one**, **nobody**, **none**, or a negative verb like **isn't** or **can't** or **won't**.

Positive sentence	Negative sentence
Peter is running.	He is **not** walking.
We should tell the truth.	We should **never** tell lies.
Everyone is in the garden.	There is **no one** in the house.
The fridge is empty.	There is **nothing** in it.
It is very cloudy.	It **isn't** sunny.
I have sold the last newspaper.	I have **no** newspapers left.
Someone has eaten all the cookies.	There are **none** in the bag.

Questions

There are two kinds of questions: yes or no questions and **wh**- questions.

4 You ask a **yes** or **no** question to get **yes** or **no** as the answer. Use the verbs **be**, **have** or **do**, or any of the helping verbs, to ask **yes** or **no** questions.

Can you swim? **Yes.**
Is it raining? **No.**

Are they coming? **No.**
May I come in? **Yes.**

4 In questions, the helping or auxiliary verbs come before the subject of the sentence. When **be** and **have** are used as ordinary verbs, they come before the subjects, too.

Statement	Question
Jim is ill today.	**Is** Jim ill today?
She has an older brother	**Has** she an older brother?
The cats want to be fed.	**Do** the cats **want** to be fed?
We should go now.	**Should** we **go** now?
It will rain tomorrow.	**Will** it **rain** tomorrow?
You may use my computer.	**May** I **use** your computer?
Kate can ride a bike.	**Can** Kate **ride** a bike?

Grammar Help

Here are some different ways of asking the same question:

Has he a sister called Jane?
Does he have a sister called Jane?
Has he got a sister called Jane?

> Wh- questions usually include the verbs **be**, **have**, **do**, or any of the helping verbs.

4 To ask for facts, use the question words **what**, **which**, **who**, **whom**, **how**, **when**, **where**. The helping verbs in **wh-** questions usually come before the subject. So does the verb **be** when it is used as an ordinary verb.

Where **are** you?

What **is** David **saying**?

How **did** you **get up** here?

Why **was** the girl **crying**?

Which color **do** you **prefer**?

Who **is** she **going to invite** to her party?

Whom **is** she **going to invite** to her party?

What **is** your problem?

When **do** the stores **open** in the morning?

Where **shall** I **put** this box?

What **have** you **done** to my computer?

How **am** I **going to finish** all this work?

What **would** you **like** for dinner?

Whose dictionary
is this?

4 If the **wh-** question word is the subject of the question, it comes before the verb. For example:

Who **told** you that?
What **made** you change your mind?

Exercise 1

Write *short answers* to the following questions.

Example: Is he tall?   Yes, <u>he is</u>.

1   Do you know the answer? Yes, _____.

2   Is Sara at home?   No, _____.

3   Do they know any grammar?   Yes, _____.

4   Are all of you coming to my house this evening?
    Yes, _____.

5   Is Mrs. Chen your English teacher?   No, _____.

6   Can you dance? No, _____.

Exercise 2

Fill in the blanks with the correct question words from the box.

where	when	why	how
whose	what	who	which

1   _____ is your house?

2   _____ wallet is this?

3   _____ are you always late?

4   _____ wrote this book?

5   _____ of the two boys is smarter?

6   _____ size do you wear?

7   _____ old is he?

8   _____ is Jeff going to get a haircut?

14 Punctuation

Punctuation marks are signs such as **periods**, **commas** and **question marks**. You use them in sentences to make the meaning clear.

Period

You put a **period** at the end of a sentence.

He drew a horse.

Albert is my good friend.

Please don't be late.

The bird is sitting on a branch.

It's snowing heavily today.

There's a rainbow in the sky.

This big house belongs to a rich man.

I can swim.

Ethan is good at drawing.

They all enjoyed playing baseball.

Comma

> Use a comma between **nouns** and **noun phrases** in a list.

I bought two apples, three oranges and some grapes.
He enjoys tennis, badminton, skating and football.
At school we study English, math, science, history and geography.

> Use commas between **adjectives** when you use several of them to describe something.

A giraffe is a tall, long-necked, long-legged animal.
He is a tall, handsome, smart and ambitious young man.

> Use a comma after **yes** and **no**, and before **please** in sentences. You also use a comma before or after the name of the person you are speaking to.

Goodbye,

No, it has stopped. Good morning, sir!
Can you tell me what time it is, please?
Yes, it's a quarter past three, George.

> Commas are used to show where there is a brief pause.

Unfortunately, she injured her knee skiing.
She was in the bedroom, listening to music on the radio.

Exclamation Point

An **exclamation point** is often used after a command, an interjection, or a word that shows **surprise** or **anger**.

Sit down!

Oh dear!

What a surprise!

You are fired!

I told you not to do that!

Quiet!

Put the knife down!

Help! Help!

Eeek! A ghost!

Stop him!

Question Mark

Use a **question mark** after a **question**.

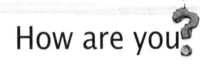

How are you?

What's your name?

How many stamps do you have?

Where do they come from?

Who has taken my pen?

Can you lend me your bicycle?

Where are you going?

Why are you always late?

What's the meaning of this word?

Do you know the answer to this problem?

Apostrophe

Use an **apostrophe** with an **s** (**'s**) to show who owns something.

The **'s** is added after singular nouns or names.

This is Peter's bed and that is Michael's bed.

A squirrel's tail is big and bushy.

We all like Mom's cooking.

Amanda clears everybody's plates after dinner.

John's dog is very friendly.

All the pupils have a month's vacation in June.

I spent the evening at David's playing video games.

I took a ride in Tom's car.

Father is holding Susie's hand.

Jane is wearing her mother's shoes.

We're going to our aunt's house.

There is a bird's nest in that tree.

Our dog's collar is brown.

Is this Portland's tallest building?

4 Follow the same rule when a name or a singular noun ends in **-s**. Write an apostrophe first and then add another **s**.

The princess's golden ball fell into a well.
A rhinoceros's skin is very thick.
Dad is at his boss's party.

4 For plural nouns that end in **-s**, put the apostrophe after the **-s**.

Birds' beaks are all different shapes and sizes.
Miss Lee is marking her pupils' work.
This is my parents' wedding photo.
Dresses are upstairs in the ladies' department.
Henry goes to a boys' school.
Dr. Kim parked his car in the doctors' parking lot.
My brothers' bedrooms are always messy.
The girls' bedrooms are usually tidy.
A flood has destroyed all the farmers' crops.

4 Some plural nouns do not end in **-s**. Just add **'s** to these plural nouns.

There are slides and swings and seesaws in the children's playground.
The men's changing room is occupied.
The bookstore sells newspapers, comics and women's magazines.
Doctors look after people's health.

4 You can also refer to **a person's office** or **shop** by using a possessive form with an apostrophe. For example:

I'll buy some bread at **the baker's.**
I was reading a book at **the dentist's.**
It's time you went to **the barber's.**

4 You can also refer to your **friends' homes** in the same way:

I'm going next door to **Peter's.** I stayed the night at **Susan's.**

4 How do you make a possessive form of two people joined by **and**, such as Peter and John, or Mary and Anne? Put **'s** only after the **second name.**

For example:

Barbara and **David's** house
Jill and **Andy's** party

4 These possessive forms of names and nouns can be used without a following noun. For example:

Which desk is **Susan's?**
George's is in the back row.
This room is **my brother's.**

> The **apostrophe** can also be used to show that one or more letters in a contraction have been left out.

I've finished my math, but I haven't finished my spelling.

We'll come to your party, but Sue won't be able to come.

He's gone to the library.

Dad wasn't at home and the children weren't at home either.

I don't like potatoes and Susan doesn't like tomatoes.

I didn't watch which way I was going and I can't find my way home.

We're late because we couldn't find your house.

Mom's finished her shopping but she hasn't gone through the checkout line yet.

Mary'd like a cat as a pet, but she wouldn't like a turtle.

You are taller than Peter, but you aren't as tall as I am.

The words **has** and **is** are often shortened to **'s** after a noun or proper noun. For example:

The mail **has** arrived.
The mail**'s** arrived.

Sally **is** here.
Sally**'s** here.

Exercise 1

Write the *punctuation marks* from the box to complete the following sentences:

> **,** **.** **?**

1   He hates cheese
2   Who is your teacher
3   Stop that man
4   Keep quiet
5   Good morning madam
6   George are you okay
7   Peter David and Susan are playing hide and seek
8   Mom bought meat fish and vegetables at the supermarket
9   What is the time now
10 Anne is a pretty girl

Exercise 2

Complete the following sentences by writing the *apostrophe(')* in the correct place:

1   This is Peters bike.
2   Paul cant find his shoes.
3   Miss Lee is marking the pupils papers.
4   They are all on the childrens playground.
5   Dont make so much noise!
6   Doctors take care of peoples health.
7   Theyre having a game of tennis.
8   Jack doesnt look well.

Printed in Great Britain
by Amazon

10158672R00093